Research and Social Change

Routledge Advances in Research Methods

Research and Social Change
A Relational Constructionist Approach

**Sheila McNamee and
Dian Marie Hosking**

Routledge
Taylor & Francis Group
NEW YORK   LONDON

First published 2012
by Routledge
711 Third Avenue, New York, NY 10017

Simultaneously published in the UK
by Routledge
2 Park Square, Milton Park, Abingdon, Oxon OX14 4RN

*Routledge is an imprint of the Taylor & Francis Group,
an informa business*

First issued in paperback 2013

Typeset in Sabon by IBT Global.

Library of Congress Cataloging-in-Publication Data
McNamee, Sheila.
   Research and social change : a relational constructionist approach /
by Sheila McNamee and Dian Marie Hosking.
      p. cm. — (Routledge advances in research methods ; 4)
   Includes bibliographical references and index.
   1. Social sciences—Research.   2. Social constructionism.   3. Social
change.   I. Hosking, Dian Marie, 1949–   II. Title.
   H62.M2337 2012
   001.4—dc23
   2011034709

ISBN13: 978-0-415-80671-8 (hbk)
ISBN13: 978-0-415-71979-7 (pbk)
ISBN13: 978-0-203-12753-7 (ebk)

Contents

Figures

Tables

Images

Preface

"Down the rabbit hole"

This volume takes a constructionist view of inquiry. Specifically, the focus is on elaborating what research and all forms of inquiry might look like within our constructionist meta-theory. We offer a wide-ranging orientation to constructionist inquiry for practitioners (managers, clinicians, educators, and consultants) who want to develop their practice and want to reflect on how their work generates useful "knowledge." We also invite students, including those who are new to research, into a view of research as a relational process.

In our work we have found that few people appreciate that research is always "with philosophy" (Bentz and Shapiro 1998, 6). Also, people often fail to recognize that they have a philosophy (often the "received view of science") and are unaware that, within the science community, there are a number of quite different philosophies. We also find that many practitioners and students (and practitioner-students) assume that theory and method are independent, assume that a method is what it is regardless of context, and assume that an interest in social construction demands qualitative methods. Happily, it is also our experience that those with whom we work are curious and excited to know more about relational constructionism (as a philosophical stance) and its possible implications for their inquiries and for (their) approaches to organizational and community development (change) work. When viewed from our relational constructionist stance, research is conceived of in different and broader terms than post-positivist (or indeed the "received view" of) science. Because research is a process of inquiry, a constructionist sensibility implies that we are all engaged in research. This does not mean that we reject (post-positivist) 'scientific' research; rather, as we will see, we reposition it as a "form of life" practiced in its own "language game" (Wittgenstein 1953), where other "forms" and "games" are also possible and have their own legitimacy.

We see this volume as being quite different from most other books about research, not least because it is not a "methods" book. To explain, our relational constructionist philosophy does not offer research methods; it offers resources that help to orient us toward inquiry in ways that *give precedence to the constitutive nature of all forms of inquiry.* One of the themes we highlight is the idea that research is an everyday activity. In the words of one of our reviewers, it is "the 'bread and butter' work of human service practitioners rather than the exclusive work of social scientists. This book is also different in that we emphasize inquiry processes oriented toward openness and making space for dissensus, complexity, and multiplicity. This orientation is unavailable and makes no sense (actually nonsense) in the context of, for example, "the received view of science" or post-positivist science.

We are also very much concerned with the 'how' of relating, generally and particularly in the context of inquiry. On the latter, post-positivist science renders the relation between 'researcher' and 'researched' as a largely technical and practical matter. It is the researcher's job to be as detached and controlled as possible so as to produce relatively objective knowledge. Our relational constructionist philosophy (or meta-theory) invites us to reflect on how positions (researcher/researched) are co-constructed. We are drawn to consider what our practices might mean for how we (always in relation) live our lives and how we might live 'a good life.' We use the term "subject-object" to speak of hierarchical, detached, knowing, and controlling ways of relating. We concentrate on exploring other, less hierarchical, more relationally engaged possibilities of co-inquiry in which knowing and influencing are more equally balanced. Our orientation toward non-hierarchical practices also is relevant to our ways of relating as co-authors. We are equal co-authors and have been on all our writing projects together. However, because local expediencies require someone's name to be first listed on the book cover, we take turns to be first named.

A WORD ON TERMINOLOGY

We have carefully chosen a particular terminology to use throughout this volume. Perhaps the most central term is "relational construction," which we choose to use rather than "social construction." We do so because there is a great deal of confusion about the latter term. Different authors and different "schools of thought" provide narratives that share a "family resemblance" (Burr 2003, 2) in their use of the term. But at the same time there are very significant differences. In addition, some writers use the term (social) construc*tivism* to speak of what others call (social) construction*ism*. And to make this yet more complicated, sometimes they mean the same thing (by the different terms) but sometimes they mean very different things. We felt that by using the term "relational" readers might be less quick to assume that they already know what we mean and might be more open to hearing the particularities of our view.

Our more substantive reason for preferring the term "relational constructionism" is because it directs attention to *relational processes* as opposed to pre-existing (individual and social) structures and their influences on how we construe the world. While Gergen's (2009b) social construction is very much focused on relational processes, many other writers situate social construction within the sociological realm, referencing Berger and Luckmann's (1966) famous book, *The Social Construction of Reality*. The term "social" is used to argue that the social world imprints or forces its powers of construction onto the (separately existing) individual. In choosing *relational* construction as the anchoring term of this volume, we are hoping to invite you into what we consider to be a "radically relational" orientation to the world. In this view, relational processes are brought 'center stage,' and both person and world are seen to emerge in these processes.

When we talk about being radically relational, we are echoing Gregory Bateson's (1972) claim that "mind is social." We are inviting you to move beyond your taken-for-granted assumptions about the boundaries among person, community, institution, or environment and see that what we take to be reality is the product of relational engagement. Relational construction is focused on how we make relational realities in relational processes, what these realities/processes constrain and potentiate, and how we might "go on together" (Wittgenstein 1953) to 'live a good life.'

While we are discussing terminology, we should say something about our use of the suffix "ism" in relational construction*ism*. When "ism" is added to the word construction, it transforms construction from an action to a thing (from a verb to a noun). However, this is not our intent. In fact, "entifying" our relational constructionist approach (i.e., making a "thing" or an "entity" out of processes) is not at all what we desire. We are writing here about a very particular stance toward the world. This stance, as you will see, emerges from some very particular assumptions about what exists, what we can know about what exists, how we can produce knowledge of what exists, and what our relationship is to the 'other'/world (what exists). Yet we do not want our stance to become dogmatic. We see relational constructionism as an orientation to the world. As such, it is perhaps better thought of not so much as a philosophy or meta-theory, but more a "way of being" or, indeed, 'becoming.' We speak of relational construct*ionism* as the moving location from which, for example, we examine any and all theoretical or methodological orientations.

Throughout this volume we have written of our relational constructionist meta-theory and our relational constructionist approach. We invite you to read both terms as "ways of talking" as opposed to representations of the world or "rules that direct action."

OUR BOOK TITLE

A word about our title and our references to research and social change: Again, this brings us to a distinctive feature of this book in that we do not find it necessary or necessarily useful to draw a hard and fast distinction between research and social change. Given our relational constructionist stance, all research intervenes in the lives of those who participate as well as in the lives of the researchers themselves. This means that professionals who work in fields focused on social change, such as health and human services, organizational development, education, and community development, are just as much *researchers* as they are change agents. Similarly, researchers are change agents; they are not simply scientists making discoveries about the world; they change the world as they examine it. Inquiry is a relational practice and (re)constructs or constitutes relational realities.

In this volume we examine research—or any inquiry/development process—as a process of construction itself. To that end, this volume is not a "how-to" book for anxious researchers; it is a book that brings the reader into the discourse of relational constructionism in such a way that the reader can examine his or her own practice as a form of inquiry. We have attempted to avoid heavy use of technical language and have included case illustrations and descriptive examples to ground and illustrate our constructionist themes and orientations. There are hundreds (or, indeed, perhaps thousands) of books on research methods. In keeping with positive science, these books emphasize 'method' and neglect meta-theoretical assumptions and interests, and they are written in ways that speak to others in the academic community. We have tried to offer something different here. We have focused on articulating relational constructionist premises, exploring these in terms of their generative possibilities for both inquiry and transformative change work. Our hope is to help a reflective practitioner or practice-oriented academic imagine his or her work as a legitimate form of research.

OUR COMMUNITY

This book emerges from the many communities in which we participate. We both identify as scholars and acknowledge that our primary professional position as university professors creates a very particular set of expectations for "success." There are certain requirements (peer reviewed publication, "significant" contributions to the field, etc.) that we must meet to "perform" as professors. At the same time, we both also inhabit the world of professional practitioners. First, we are educators and "practice" our trade every day in the classroom. Yet we also work as consultants, supervisors, and evaluators inside and outside of the university. We view our various constructed identities as scholars and practitioners as important to our work. We feel privileged to work with groups, communities, institutions, organizations, and cultures in ways that help us put our relational constructionist orientation to work. We also feel privileged to occupy positions where writing 'about' the ways we work can contribute to the academy and generate further ways of knowing and understanding.

We have been fortunate to be involved with colleagues who are devoted to relational understandings of the world and who, themselves, have devoted their professional lives to creating innovative forms of relational constructionist practice—both within and beyond the academy. Of particular note is our global community of colleagues affiliated with the Taos Institute of which Sheila is a founder and Dian Marie an associate. These colleagues and good friends sustain our commitment and passion for our work and inspire us with their creativity and inventive practices. We also have drawn heavily from the performative practices inspired by our colleagues at the East Side Institute in New York City. This is a group with whom we always feel very much at home. Other streams and configurations where we have learned and always gained support and provocations include the community of systemic practitioners, organization development and consulting groups around the world, and our academic colleagues in communication studies, social psychology, the philosophy of inquiry, organization studies, critical theory, performance studies, and cultural studies. To all these communities—our web of relations—we owe much gratitude for the ways in which we have been inspired to create alternative understandings of research and professional practice.

Also, it would be most remiss of us if we failed to thank the many people who generously contributed their time and expertise to give us invaluable feedback and abundant support for this project. They include James Day, Janice DeFehr, Rodney Merrill, Ellen Raboin, Maggie Shelton, and Stephen Shimshock, together with other reviewers whose names we do not know; we are grateful to you all for your careful comments and suggestions. We offer a very special thanks to our undergraduate and postgraduate students whose readiness to live with the newness and uncertainties have been vital in allowing us to learn how to teach this challenging material. We also want to thank our workshop participants (students, practitioners, and student-practitioners) who have provided cases, illustrations, and stories. We believe (and hope) that, as a reader of this book, you will be able to see your own doubts and uncertainties about "research" in their cases, illustrations, and stories. We also hope that you are inspired by their ways of working through their own lack of confidence. A very special thanks goes to Celiane Camargo-Borges and Murilo Moscheta who took time to read this manuscript and share their very creative ideas with us.

The quotes that serve as subtitles for each chapter heading are taken from Lewis Carroll's classic tale of *Alice in Wonderland*. The photographs were taken by Celiane Camargo-Borges at the Utrecht School of Governance, Utrecht University, Utrecht, The Netherlands. We thank Celiane for allowing us to use her photographs. Finally, no acknowledgment can be complete without recognizing the patience and support of our families: Sage, Follie, Taylor, and Jack—all who waited for meals, for walks, and for play time while we worked endlessly on this book!

1 Inquiry Possibilities

"Why is a raven like a writing desk?"

INQUIRY AS CONSTRUCTION

In this chapter we introduce a constructionist stance toward research and social change. Our aim is to raise questions about how research is understood and how one might engage in the process of research within a relational constructionist stance. Specifically, we are interested in opening up the sacred domain of research—that domain frequently understood as occupied only by scientists—to illustrate how the everyday practices of consultants, change agents, educators, and a whole host of professionals qualify as research.

We make this argument from within a very particular discursive space, the space of what we call relational constructionism. Although we could easily identify our orientation as social construction, we believe the term "relational construction" more adequately identifies the philosophical stance we take and also helps us highlight the precise understanding we have of social construction. Social construction is often conflated with versions of constructivism (radical constructivism, social constructivism) where the focus is on how interaction in the social milieu constructs internal knowledge. There are also versions of social construction that are purely language-based, where interest is limited to the ways in which words construct realities.

Our own orientation will become clear as this volume unfolds (in particular, see Chapter 3). For now, let us simply orient you to our relational constructionist stance by saying that we are focused on *relational processes* and the ways in which these processes construct various forms of life. We do not concern ourselves with individual mental processes or individual traits and characteristics. Rather, our focus is on what people do together and what their "doing" makes.

We regularly run workshops focused on the theme of this book. Many of our workshop participants are working on a Ph.D. from a relational constructionist perspective and want to learn more about what this could mean for their inquiry methods, design, analysis, and report. When we first meet, we ask them to write a brief description of their work—one that could bring us into a conversation with them about how they can move forward in generative and useful ways. Here is one such description from Temi, a man working in Nairobi, Kenya.

Challenges of Working with a Community of HIV/AIDS Care Givers

It's a Saturday morning in a remote rural town called Migwani. The town is located some 200 km to the east of the capital city of Nairobi and is the administrative headquarters of the Migwani division. The division has a population of about one hundred thousand people and is divided into seven administrative locations with each location being further sub-divided into between five and nine sub-locations.

It is barely ten o'clock in the morning, yet on this particular day, the menacing African sun is already too hot to bear. As I step out of my car, a couple of businesswomen, who hawk ripe bananas for a living, approach and we exchange pleasantries.

It is from these ladies that I hear the sad news that Mutunga passed away three days ago and is being buried today. In that instant, all of my plans for the day are completely changed. Mutunga was one of my most ardent HIV/AIDS community educators and was scheduled to give a talk on "positive living" in a workshop I was to hold today for leaders of the HIV/AIDS community of care in a neighboring village. A cheerful fellow who used to work in the coastal city of Mombasa until 2002, Mutunga was fired by his employer for being sick most of the time and missing work.

Upon returning to the village, he invested his last earnings in a small retail shop in Migwani town. Yet, after only one year, the business failed. While Mutugna's health had somewhat improved, the health of his wife and five year old—and youngest—daughter were on the decline. In December 2005, his last-born daughter passed away, followed by his wife within the same month. Mutunga was devastated. It was the story of the entire area. Mutunga's family had been bewitched, and unless something was done and done very quickly, the entire family would disappear soon.

I heard the story of the sad demise of Mutunga's family during the Christmas holidays of 2006. I asked one of the board members of our community organization to ask Mutanga to get in touch with me the following weekend. Sure enough, Mutunga came to see me at my rural home the following Saturday very early in the morning. This is when I learned that he was 40 years old and had been working as a waiter with a leading tourist hotel at the coastal city of Mombasa for fifteen years but had been fired in 2002 when he became ill. He told me that he had been tested for all kinds of illness except HIV/AIDS.

I also learned from him that he was the first born in a family of nine, six girls and three boys. Three of the girls had been doing odd jobs in Mombasa where they contracted some mysterious ailments, and all had died, leaving him with the extra burden of taking care of six orphaned nieces and nephews. However, after the shocking demise of his youngest daughter and wife, he was ready to do anything to stay alive and take care of his remaining six children as well as his late sisters' children.

After listening to Mutunga for about three hours, I came to the conclusion that he had all the symptoms of HIV/AIDS but was too frightened to go for testing. His fear was the product of the stigma associated with the disease. I assured him of my total confidentiality and support as well as that of Omega Child Shelter, a local community-based organization that I, together with some friends, started in 2002 for the sole purpose of initiating local, sustainable HIV/AIDS coping mechanisms among the infected and the affected. Today, the organization is giving direct support to well over 500 children orphaned by HIV/AIDS and well over 150 people living with AIDS within our program area.

Our field coordinator made the necessary arrangements, and Mutunga was able to travel to Muthale Mission hospital the following Monday for HIV/AIDS testing and counseling. The test results confirmed our worst fears. Mutunga was not only HIV/AIDS positive but his T-cell count was dangerously low. Mutunga was immediately put on anti-retroviral drugs. He was also enlisted into our newly formed psychosocial counseling and support group for people living with AIDS and willing to live positively with the disease.

Within a period of about six months, Mutunga went public about his HIV/AIDS status following which we sponsored him for several courses on holistic post-HIV/AIDS management. Going public about his status was a milestone of sorts because, until then, the disease had been a complete stigma within the community. Following his disclosure, the disease was being openly discussed as an unfortunate condition that no one could cure. However, discussion was now focused on how one might live positively with such an incurable disease.

Soon, we appointed Mutunga to head our special unit, which was moving from school to school teaching young boys and girls of the dangers of early and unprotected sex, HIV/AIDS management, and training and counseling of care giver groups. He was the most sought-after public speaker in virtually all forums where people needed to be educated about the HIV/AIDS pandemic.

But now, Mutunga is no more. He is gone. And, as I get back into my car to drive the eight or so kilometers to Mutunga's home, I cannot stop wondering almost out loud about a number of critical issues: *Why now? Where the hell are we going to get another charming, eloquent, convincing team leader like him? How are we going to deal with his orphaned children as well as those of his late sisters, all of whom we must now care for?*

As I drive into Mutunga's compound, I cannot avoid noticing the thousands of mourners, young and old, who have come to pay their last respects to a man who, partly due to fate and partly because of his condition, had touched so many souls within such a relatively short period of time. As I park my car, I cannot stop wondering, *why now?* Is there somewhere I could make an appeal to have him back—even if only for a few more years?

When we read Temi's story, we were deeply touched. Mutunga's situation raises many questions about public health, community, and care. Temi's story, while also raising these same questions, invites us to think about how we, as consultants, researchers, and change agents, can work *with* people to create possibilities for social transformation; this was Temi's concern. For example, he was interested in exploring how he could conduct research with the communities in which he was engaged. For whom should the work be done and for what purposes or interests? How can the quality of the work be evaluated? Could and should work of this sort still be called "research" or might other terms be more helpful? And, perhaps most pressing for Temi was the commonly experienced insecurity that the work he was doing in this community, as in others, could not be considered 'research.'

OPENING "INQUIRIES"

Temi is one of many student-practitioners with whom we work. Practitioners' fields of practice include government or public services, community and international development, healthcare, organizational consulting, education, and counseling and therapy. We have found that such persons often view "research" as something only scientists do. It is for this and other reasons that we have shifted to the more everyday term "inquiry." The term "inquiry" can seem more a part of the daily practices of those who do not think of themselves as scientists and it gives space to activities that some views of science would not count as scientific. For us, and for those with whom we work, the term "inquiry" seems to imply an orientation toward exploration and opening up to the senses along with a curiosity and openness to what might be. The term "science," in contrast, is often understood to imply the use of a reliable method or technique for objectively discovering how things are. We will have more to say about this, particularly in Chapter 2.

The 'everyday-ness' of the term "inquiry" also seems to connect with the daily activity of reflection. People with whom we work often speak of their reflective orientation toward their own practice as managers, consultants, therapists, educators, and other professionals. Many of them want to make reflection a central feature of their master's or doctoral theses, or of their professional practice. In other words, they want to make their own practice the subject of their inquiry rather than, for example, contriving special situations for the purposes of data collection. This desire to reflect on practice is gaining widespread attention; we see this as an illustration of what Donald Schön (1983, 10) refers to as a "reflective practitioner" approach.

Yet practitioners are not the only ones who feel that research is something only scientists do. Students—at both the undergraduate and graduate levels—commonly share a narrow view of research, one that is circumscribed by the discourse of post-positivist science. To us, this unreflective view severely limits students' (as well as practitioners') abilities to orient their inquiry from the questions and issues that engage them and that they would be eager to explore in more detail. We find that using the term 'inquiry' invites those new to research into a more generous space.

From now on, we will use the term "inquiry" very broadly to include the interests and practices that certain communities would call research. Of course, different communities have very different ideas or "meta-theories" about what counts as research. Because we are writing this text from the standpoint of relational constructionism, we will focus on the interests and practices that this particular community allows, invites, and legitimizes. In this book we outline practical features of constructionist-inspired inquiry including: the blurring of boundaries between inquiry and daily life, an emphasis on process, and a general orientation toward openness and multiplicity, appreciation and relational engagement.

OPENING UP TO MULTIPLE, COMMUNITY-BASED CONSTRUCTIONS OF INQUIRY

Perhaps now is a good moment to say that, even within the social sciences, it is possible to identify multiple communities characterized by different social science perspectives. More than forty years ago, Thomas Kuhn (1970) spoke of multiple "coherent traditions of scientific research," each being characterized by a bundle of interrelated but different assumptions, different interests, and different ways of doing things. He further suggested that identification with a particular "tradition" is effectively a matter of becoming a member of a *particular* professional community. Although Kuhn spoke of traditions succeeding one another, recent years have witnessed the emergence of multiple co-existing research "traditions."

The simultaneous presence of different traditions with different norms, values, and interests (meta-theories) suggests the need to closely consider and be sensitive to the different coherences that define each tradition. Without such sensitivity there is the risk that one set of community-based constructions may dominate, mute, obscure, or devalue practices that have their own different intelligibility in relation to a different tradition. As we have said, it is our intention to focus this book on a *relational constructionist* tradition, meta-theory, or "intelligibility." One of the defining qualities of this tradition is that it centers relational processes and relational realities. We begin with the notion that relational processes construct particular, local-historical, community-based understandings. To begin from this presumption suggests that we also acknowledge that other communities are engaged in similar processes whereby they may construct very different particularities. We have much more to say about this in Chapter 2.

Reflexively applying this orientation to the writing of this book reminds us of one of our reasons for writing it. Perhaps we can illustrate this with a story about the most recent piece of writing we did together. We were responding to a call for papers for a special issue of a practitioner journal whose focus is Appreciative Inquiry (AI) (http://www.aipractitioner. com/). The call noted that AI is often evaluated in relation to traditional scientific norms, values, and interests and that, when judged in this context, is usually found wanting. Commonly voiced criticisms included lack of rigor, lack of control, lack of quantitative and shown-to-be-reliable and valid data concerning outcomes, and so on. For these and related issues, the editors wanted a special issue that focused on the question, "How does AI change the way we do research and think about it?" Our response was to write an article setting out relational constructionist premises, tracing their interrelations (coherence), and showing how these were reflected in the practices and purposes of AI (Hosking and McNamee 2007). Our purpose was not to argue for the superiority of a relational constructionist sensibility. Rather, our attempt was to invite critics of AI to consider the relational, process orientation that guides this work and that provides the context within which the quality of AI should rightly be judged (Haar and Hosking 2004).

(RE)CONSTRUCTING NON-HIERARCHICAL RELATIONS AMONG MULTIPLE FORMS OF LIFE

The human or social sciences are often identified as having a way of knowing (one way) that is superior to other ways of knowing. Scientific knowledge is constructed as reliable, valid, and generalizable. As such, it is commonly viewed as constituting the rational basis for design (e.g., organizational structuring) and intervention (e.g., new, more effective working practices). However, our relational constructionist tradition offers no basis for privileging any one 'form of life' (Wittgenstein 1953) over others. In this view, science (of whatever tradition) is not necessarily privileged over other local community-based constructions.

In short, inquiry *need not* be designed and justified in relation to the norms and standards of what people might think of as science. Indeed, relational constructionist premises invite *openness to possibilities* rather than closure or critique that routinely valorizes one tradition over others. Relational constructionist premises invite practices that are open to the multiple, different, more or less local norms and values of the *many* communities involved in some inquiry and not just those of the scientific community. This brings us to a key aspect of our relational stance—that such practices require a shift in relations. A shift is required in how we understand the "position" of the researcher (as expert or as collaborator, for example) and the "researched" (as research objects or as co-constructors). Now we are faced with the puzzle of what inquiry can become when a researcher does *not* attempt to relate to other as a potentially knowable and formable object in subject-object relation. To put the question in slightly different terms: How can inquiry practices make space for multiple communities to shape inquiry purposes, methods, and forms of reporting? This issue is the central theme of this book.

Our point is *not* that all inquiry has to do this. Rather, we are interested to create space for and to explore possibilities that make no sense or are viewed as nonsense in a more conventional science tradition. These are practices that can be developed through attempts to amplify the equal legitimacy of *all* participating communities' norms, values, and interests.

Perhaps a short story will help to illustrate. This one comes from work done by Dian Marie and her colleague David Crowther during the last foot and mouth epidemic in the UK. They explored the ways in which web-based media were used to articulate views and summon support for particular constructions and interests. They soon found that various government websites were used to make official statements about what was happening. In the case of these sites, the style and tone were factual and informative. Quantitative data were presented as facts about what was happening and as justifications for government policy and practices such as closure of large parts of the countryside and the mass culling of animals. In addition, and through exploring other websites and media statements, it gradually became clear that different scientists had very different views about what was and was not a fact, as did other community spokespersons, including farmers, bed and breakfast owners, and restaurant owners.

At a certain point, the government claimed warrant for an especially legitimate voice. They constructed official "*government* scientists" whose facts were apparently better than those of non-government scientists and, naturally, better than those of non-scientists. Government decision makers attached greater value to quantitative data along with methods such as computer-based modeling. Narrative accounts of personal experiences and local interests were devalued as parochial, subjective, emotional, and biased, rather than objective and 'for the general good' (Crowther and Hosking 2005).

Returning to our reflective practitioners and their approaches to inquiry, the relational constructionist premises invite us all to reflect on the community-based constructions we put to work in our inquiries. Our concern here is in exploring practices of inquiry that are less likely to be associated with common notions of "science."

Reflection

In Dian Marie's story, the scientifically accepted language of computer models and quantitative data were privileged. We are interested in exploring how we might consider questions that might include the following:

- *Does my inquiry need to further my career and/or enable me to get a Ph.D. or a promotion (or, who is this research for, anyway)?*
- *Do I want to practice in ways that could be open to and appreciative of multiple, local community-based constructions (or, am I the only one who could possibly make "research decisions" about this topic)?*
- *Do I already have some issue with which I have a personal or 'heart connection' that I want to investigate in some way (or, how do my own interests and values—my life story—"show up" in this research)?*
- *Do I see a sharp distinction between inquiry and intervention, between science and consulting (or, if my inquiry helps and changes people—including myself—can't it still be viewed as "research")?*

Answers to these questions have considerable relevance for how we think about inquiry and what might be possible given the particularities of the multiple communities or forms of life with which we work.

An illustration of these considerations is provided by the following case from Femke, a participant in one of our workshops. We asked all participants to write about a practice setting that raised questions of inquiry and intervention for them. Our idea was that these questions would not only focus the workshop toward participants' needs but also make our discussion generative.

LIFE COURSE POLICIES

My Assignment

'GO' is an institutionalized consultative body in the sweets, chocolate, and biscuit industry. It consists of delegates of three main labor unions and some employers. It prepares and agrees on the collective labor agreements on behalf of the grass roots members. They appointed a working group to research the possibilities of Sustainable Life Course Policies. Three consulting bureaus, including my own (LifeCo), made proposals for this work. LifeCo has contributed a lot to raising awareness about this issue in The Netherlands, and we are now developing forms of implementation with our clients.

LifeCo's Project Proposal

We noted that, in our experience, most employers have awareness of issues associated with an aging labor force and of the increasingly aging population. However, employers do not necessarily have ways of dealing with what this means for their enterprise or how to manage these developments. We proposed that if you really want to make change within organizations, you have to start a dialogue with everyone involved: MT, HR-manager, works council, and employees. LifeCo was chosen for the project, and, after a further orienting meeting with the secretary of the work group, we made a proposal. The main questions for our inquiry became:

- How can employees in this industry, especially the operators, become and remain employable?
- What steps must the employers take to enable their employees to take responsibility for their individual, enduring employability?

Reflections: Some Lines Out of My Journal

My colleague was very surprised—you start your proposal with a desired situation. . . .

The working group wants a 'cut' between research and analysis and implementation (I hate that word), I totally forgot to make a 'cut' because for me there is no 'cut,' nobody reminded me of this request that I never responded to, actually, I totally forgot about this remark when writing the final proposal. . . .

About the focus groups (group interviews with employees): some members of the working group doubt if the 'results'—the insights— will be transferable to the whole branch. . . . I find it very difficult to convince them or to share with them my belief that listening to the people involved will bring us the desired dialogue and the needed steps to be taken.

I want lots more time for business visits—to get in touch and build relationships with the companies. I get so happy to get in touch with the Manufacturers. The HR-managers make time to have a bit of exchange after the visit. I feel that the HR-managers like to sit with a cup of tea and to have a talk.

I experience, at the moment, little commitment of the members of the working group. I have to raise this at the next meeting. This will delay the planning, but more important, I cannot do their work. . . .

My biggest attention and concern goes to the members of the work group. Busy as the HR-managers are with the business or the governors of the labor unions with governing, I want to remind them that their commitment to start the changes they are aiming for is needed.

My Interest . . .

I got to know Dian at the USBO in 2005. I was one of the lecturers in her course on Qualitative Inquiry in the 2nd year. What fun! Unfortunately, some months later I left for a sabbatical abroad, but not before consulting Dian. So I added some new titles to the pile of books I wanted to read in the time that was in front of me. I had collected some authors whose work I wanted to read such as Hutton and Armstrong about Group Relations/Organization in the Mind and Assagioli and Ferrucci on Psycho Synthesis. Dian added Berman, Newman, and Holzman and later on Anderson.

That year I enjoyed reading. I made up my mind about the difference between Psycho Analysis and Psycho Synthesis, never wrote an article, decided not to go back to teaching, but started to look for a job preferably in which I could support the self-agency of individuals within organizations. Real listening, real dialogue, and working from a philosophical stance like Anderson writes about and practices—these were key practices.

Back in The Netherlands, I started to work and totally lost track of all the promising and inviting theories and stories I had read. One important reason for this was that the company I work for is (up until now) known for its research and analysis projects that, in my point of view, have little to do with change work. So it took me time to get a project organized in which I would be able to do what I aim to do. When I started the project on life course trajectories, it was about time for a consultation, and I visited Dian's site and this workshop popped up, so the circle is round. . . .

Femke's story highlights some of the many themes that become apparent when working from a relational constructionist orientation. These themes include (1) the ways in which inquiry implicates relationships, life situations, and conversations; (2) the possibility for a research project to emerge from the ordinary flux and flow of daily life; and (3) the possibility of any relational practice to lean toward inquiry or transformation.

Different assumptions about relations between inquiry and intervention and the relative value of appreciation versus critique are illustrated by another story, this time from Sheila. Her story concerns the evaluation of a high school academic program. She was invited to work with one academic department of a prestigious, private high school. The entire school had been charged with revising the curriculum. And, given the contentious nature of interpersonal/professional relationships among the staff in one particular department, the department head saw the curriculum revision process as the perfect opportunity to call in an outside consultant. As the outside consultant, Sheila was formally asked to help the staff assess and revise their program. Informally, she was asked to improve their working relations.

Sheila's introduction to the staff occurred at the first faculty meeting of the academic year. During this introduction, she explained that her intention was not to conduct research on them and not to evaluate their program and working style but rather to invite them into a conversation. She described her interest in working from discussions of what they valued in their program and in their collegial relationships as opposed to engaging in detailed explorations of what was not working or what they did not like. She further articulated that her attempt would be to bracket earlier and current discussions of problems and blame and instead focus on how to build on the curricular and collegial *strengths* that already were acknowledged. Further, she explained that her intention was not to find a way to make them like one another. Rather, her hope was that the process of their collaborative evaluation would generate respect for differences. In addition, she hoped that the department would begin to develop more collaborative, respectful working relations by virtue of their participation in the joint creation of the evaluation.

The details of this work are described elsewhere (McNamee 2004a). One interesting feature of this work is the debate that followed publication. The latter was written as an illustration of how to conduct program evaluation in a collaborative, appreciative manner. The debate initiated by the publication of this case concerned the distinction between evaluation research and consultation. To the journal editors, the article was an illustration of consultancy work not of program evaluation. To Sheila, the case illustrated the value of consultancy as a transformative process (Reed 2007). From a relational constructionist view, consultants engage with participants to construct and transform the program. This story illustrates again the important distinction we make between inquiry as a relational process that cannot avoid participating in its own "outcome" and inquiry (scientific research) as a procedure for discovery. This volume will explore this theme in detail.

Thus far we have offered several illustrations of professional practitioners' work as a form of inquiry. Yet this volume is not written solely for practitioners. We are also interested in introducing students who are new to research to a rich sense of constructionist inquiry. In our own experience as students (as well as in our experience with our students), we recognize the doubt, fear, and anxiety that accompany any first attempt at research. While practitioners (professionals) might feel de-authorized as researchers because they have been told that investigation (research) and intervention (professional practice) should remain discrete, students feel de-authorized as researchers because they have been told that a "good" researcher "knows ahead of time." Also, students are taught to distinguish between method and practice, data and data analysis. The following story illustrates one Ph.D. student's struggle to think of himself as a researcher.

MURILO'S STORY

Murilo was interested in understanding how healthcare professionals understand and work with GLBT (gay, lesbian, bisexual, transgender) patients. He carefully designed his research to include (1) an open invitation to professionals in one health center to participate in his project, (2) one-on-one interviews with those who volunteered for participation to gain a sense of their challenges in working with GLBT patients, and (3) a series of open dialogues with all participants.

All was going quite smoothly in his research; he had a good number of volunteers and completed his one-on-one interviews. He carefully prepared for his first dialogue session with the health professionals by summarizing the questions and concerns voiced in the interviews. He wanted to create an open and welcoming atmosphere and so, on the day of the group dialogue, when a nurse assistant who had not previously volunteered for the project (nor had she been interviewed) asked if she could join, the answer was, "of course!" Murilo felt he was honoring the "local-emergent" practices of the healthcare professionals. However, to his horror, the newly joining nurse assistant abruptly left the dialogue session when she realized that everyone else present had participate in a personal interview. She felt marginalized.

Murilo felt that his research was a disaster at this point until he made the decision to seek out the nurse assistant and ask her if she would like to join the group. This decision opened a new horizon of possibilities in his research: Participants collaborated intensely, and the group used the "unfortunate" event as a model to think about the challenges in the inclusion of GLBT clients in healthcare settings. Not only did Murilo achieve an emergent quality to his research design and method, but also he was able to see the implications of his own research process for the topic of his research (work with GLBT clients). Later he would reflect on this research experience and highlight the transformative potential of, as he describes it, his encounter with "the unexpected":

I believe that, until that time, a great part of my training as a researcher had been based on a clear right/wrong division. The tradition in which I was trained emphasized that a good researcher would be able to carefully plan how the research should go and to anticipate possible problems in order to take suitable precautions. For omniscient pursuers like me, doubts and surprises were problems to avoid, solve, or fix. Method was a way of ensuring that everything would flow as planned. Above all, researching was about controlling. And, as daunting as this god-like position could be, it was also seductive once it waved to the possibility of joining a selected and socially appreciated group.

So it is not surprising that I would feel devastated when something unexpected happened during my research. I was striving to do everything right and, because this perspective on research is so widely acknowledged, participants were also expecting me to make "all the 'right' decisions." Therefore, I first understood the unexpected as a sign of personal failure. In my efforts for perfection, my failure was later transformed into the nursing assistant's failure, as I tried to justify myself by accusing her of disturbing my research. So my first lesson in this experience was to realize that blame is the standard game in a right/wrong model of individual responsibility. Unfortunately, that is the game that so commonly prevented me from generously understanding the unexpected and learning from it. Once I did so, the possibility of escaping the blame game allowed me to reconsider research in two important aspects.

First, I reconnected with the basic element of research. For some researchers research is about discovering what is new, whereas for some others it may be more like creating something new. However, in any case, it seems that research is a process by which we somehow create the conditions where we can be in relation with novelty. So what is the point of anticipating and controlling everything? How much space is left for "the original" if I am obsessed with predictions? I've realized that welcoming the unexpected can be a way of learning about what I was looking for without knowing I was looking for it. Paraphrasing T. S. Eliot, research can be about finding what I was looking for and knowing it for the first time. Most important, this perspective liberated me from knowing everything and encouraged a lot of exploration. The blame game gave space for playful curiosity, generous questioning, and exciting cooperation. Researching was elevated back to what it was when I first became interested in it: an adventure full of surprises for a boy playing with bugs and lenses in the backyard.

Second, I've learned that method is a compass, not a map. I was accustomed to the commonly accepted idea that relates to method as a process. However, the way I was embracing this process was transforming it into a product. I had planned interviews, I had prepared participants, and I had designed a group dialogue. And all this was a tool I wanted to apply in my research context. However, if method is truly a process, it is always in response to whatever is emerging in the research. So the most important aspect of method for me is not what I plan to do or the tools I want to use but how I respond to whatever emerges from them. Like a traveller with a compass, I can move toward one direction. But to get there, I need to be attentive and responsive to the signs I find in my way. How I get to my goal is more a matter of how I interact with both compass and signs than a matter of following the right track. Obviously that does not exclude preparation and planning, for I still do a lot of it before entering any research field or starting any trip. However, it allows me to be responsive to the unfolding nature of researching. Besides that, I consider the ethical importance of inviting participants not only to collaborate with what I propose but also to engage in the collective construction of the research process. I had heard social researchers frequently say that they were open to learn from the participants. So was I as I started my research. However, the collaboration I was expecting was restricted to the content of my research. I assumed that it was up to me, the researcher, to decide about the process and to demonstrate mastery of methodological and analytical strategies. The event was embarrassing because it suggested that I could not know how to conduct the research process. However, it was exactly because I didn't know that participants could feel invited to collaborate. Power relations were transformed and authorship could be democratized. (Moscheta 2011)

We have spoken of our orientation to relationally engaged forms of practice that are open to and appreciative of multiplicity. We will go on to show that this requires the re-unification of many forced separations such as description and construction, fact and value, body (heart)/mind, knowledge and power, inquiry and intervention, data collection and data analysis, researcher and researched, process and outcome. Of course these distinctions have long been constructed as problematic when viewed as binary opposites. One approach to the 'problem' is to continue with science and talk of scientific truth as probable, contingent, and pragmatic; another is to explore what can come out of work that orients toward:

- **Openness** including holding the space for multiple community-based constructions, relating to all community-based rationalities as always in process, and possible futures rather than past and problems;
- **Appreciation** including relating to local rationalities as having their own coherence and possibilities, relating to these with curiosity and without judgment, and opening conversation on what is valued and working;
- **Relationally engaged practice** including working in ways that are connected rather than detached and unfeeling—in ways that recognize and value inter-related rather than separate existences.

In the following chapter, we address the issue of multiplicity within the human sciences. We introduce the idea of different meta-theories as characterized by different sets of assumptions, out of which very different theories and, in turn, very different inquiry methods emerge. We also provide a context for understanding relational constructionism against the backdrop of more traditional human science perspectives and the potential implications for inquiry and transformation work that relational constructionism offers.

2 Meta-Theories and Discourses of Construction

"Goodbye feet"

WHY RELATIONAL CONSTRUCTIONISM? WHY INQUIRY?

We are guessing that you feel some connection with relational constructionism and with some of the issues we have mentioned in Chapter 1 or you would not be reading this book. This immediately raises questions about what *you* understand by relational constructionism and why you are interested in it. We have found that it can be helpful to draw distinctions between differing social science perspectives, and the differing implications these have for the what, why, and how of inquiry. Our experience has been that it is vitally important to gain some clarity on this issue, in terms of both theory and social science perspective, not least because different formalizations invite rather different practices, norms, values, and justifications.

There are many ways to engage and experience the distinction among varying social science perspectives. Each emerges (or has emerged) within a different community, informed and influenced by different assumptions and values. Relational constructionism explores the ways in which differences in assumptions generate different forms of practice.

To try this idea on, imagine yourself sitting in a room with ten other people. The room is a typical university classroom. You are an interior designer. As you look around the room you are disturbingly aware of the unattractive wall color, the old, worn-out linoleum flooring, the broken, uncomfortable chairs, and the bare walls. Sitting next to you is a fire fighter. As he situates himself in his chair, he cannot help but notice that the windows are sealed shut and there is no sprinkler system installed in the ceiling should a fire break out. He sees the room as a very dangerous place to be. Next to the fire fighter is an ecologist. As she looks around the room she cannot help but wonder if the walls have been painted with lead paint and if the janitorial staff have been sweeping lead dust off the floor for years. She sees the room as a significant health threat, and she also notices that the room is lit with highly inefficient light bulbs, adding further to global warming. Each of the others in the room brings his or her unique orientation to the room's description.

This imaginary exercise is something that we invite our workshop participants and students to explore becausee it produces very different community-based constructions of what is 'real and good' (Cottor et al. 2004). If you were to share your description of the room with others in this imaginary situation, you would probably be quite surprised by the differences. Descriptions differ, for example, in *what* is talked about (paying attention to some things and not others), in *the ways* those things are talked about (nice to look at, a fire hazard, unhealthy, and so on), and in the ways people *story their relationship* with those things (e.g., because I'm an interior designer, style and ambiance matter most to me). We use this exercise as a metaphor for differences in meta-theories. We are interested in showing that we all, always, 'see' the world from somewhere, on the basis of particular assumptions, and that there are different sets of assumptions, each with its own coherence. To take a relational constructionist approach is to adopt a particular meta-theory that then informs all our inquiry practices. In other words, relational constructionism provides an abiding and ongoing orientation in and to practice.

Reflection

If you think about the activity just described in relation to your own understanding of research, how would you answer the following questions?

- *If you are to be considered a legitimate researcher, what requirements must you meet? Could there be other requirements that others acknowledge?*
- *What are your own expectations for legitimate research? Could there be others?*
- *Where do these come from?*
- *How do these images differ from your daily professional practice?*
- *In what ways does thinking about yourself as a researcher demand you ask different questions and engage in different practices in your work?*

MULTIPLICITY WITHIN THE HUMAN SCIENCES

Different meta-theories of social science have been spoken of as "paradigms" (Kuhn 1970), "thought styles" (Fleck 1979), "discourses," "social science perspectives" (Alvesson and Deetz 2000; Deetz 1996), and "intelligibility nuclei" (Gergen 1994). Each of these terms has a history, has been developed in relation to rather different issues and interests, and has importantly different implications. Given our current purposes, these differences are too complex and nuanced to be discussed, and we suggest you look at the above referenced works for the finer detail. Whichever term we use, our intention is to refer to a bundle of interrelated distinctions that go together to make up a community-based discourse about what exists, what can be known, and how. These different discourses provide very different contexts, for example, for theories, for the ways "construction" is theorized, for inquiry methods, and for the values and interests that inquiry is assumed to serve.

Meta-theories of science differ not only in their assumptions about ontology, epistemology, and methodology but also in what they feature as the (scientific) interest and in the ways they handle the issue of quality. Probably the discourse with which you are most familiar is the one that sees science as a very particular sort of activity (controlled, repeatable, and reflexive) that produces generalizable knowledge claims that are open to a particular sort of justification. In this view, knowledge is described and defined as "justified true belief" (Hollis 1994, 9)—where the justification takes the form of empirical data that support the claims made.

But there are other forms of practice, other interests, and other justifications. We guess that many of our readers find empirical justifications grounded in scientific procedures and expressed in numbers more persuasive than, for example, 'I read it in the entrails of the goat we sacrificed this morning.' Of course you might regard this as an extreme example. But what does or can it mean to do a piece of social science inquiry and what makes it 'science'? To give you some help with this, we will begin by outlining a common discourse of science.

AN OUTLINE OF THE "RECEIVED VIEW OF SCIENCE"

The "received view of science" (RVS) is described by Steve Woolgar (1996) as one that is often presented (a) by scientists (b) in particular contexts (c) for particular audiences. For example, the RVS may be presented in introductory textbooks and in popularized accounts of science. Scientists' public declarations of science's "supposed virtues" are also likely to reflect this "received view." We have found that those new to social science also often tend to make similar assumptions; what about you?

Reflection

- *In your own inquiry, what are your main concepts (ontology)?*
- *How do you or can you know about them (epistemology)?*
- *How do you check the quality of your knowledge claims (methodology)?*
- *How do you persuade others that your knowledge is true? What lends authority to your inquiry and the "product" of that inquiry (analysis)?*

How do your reflections relate to the RVS? Let's see. In articulating the received view of science, Woolgar identifies four interrelated themes. The first concerns assumptions about the world and its components. The RVS discourse involves speaking or writing in a way that refers to a natural world made up of humans and other objects. In this context, objects are understood to exist independently of their connections or ways of relating. So, for example, leadership or expertise (concepts, see above) would be seen as measurable, objective qualities or actions of a person rather than an ongoing relation. This discourse suggests that there is one 'real reality' that is self-existing and available for science to know; philosophers of inquiry refer to this as the *assumption of ontology*.

Assumptions about what exists go together with assumptions about what we may know (in this case, scientifically) of such an existence. This brings us to the second theme of the RVS that philosophers of inquiry refer to as the *assumption of epistemology*. According to Woolgar, the RVS articulates scientific knowledge as knowledge that is determined by the characteristics of real-world objects. In other words, scientific knowledge is described as objective (about objects in the world) rather than subjective (about the object but also reflecting the idiosyncrasies of the knower making the knowledge claim). Thus, according to the RVS, we can *know about* (about-ness knowledge), for example, leadership and expertise, and we can know objectively.

The third theme deals with the issue of how knowledge can be produced; this is the *assumption of methodology*. The RVS presents this as the question of how science can produce objective knowledge. This brings us to what an introductory science course or textbook might emphasize. The received view of science gives considerable emphasis to the existence and the importance of a generally agreed set of methods, rules, and procedures. In other words, it is suggested that scientists know how to do science, that they share a high degree of consensus about this, and they believe that designing and following a scientific methodology can produce (relatively) objective knowledge.

Last, the received view of science suggests that *scientists 'do science' through individual acts of thinking, reasoning, and deciding*. In other words, the discourse implies that science is grounded in "individualistic and mentalistic" activity (Woolgar 1996, 13). These (assumed) cognitive acts (of the scientist) then are reflected in individual behaviors, such as the design and conduct of the inquiry procedure, and further put to work in the analysis and presentation of what are referred to as data.

We want to emphasize that this is the way in which (some) people sometimes *talk and/or write about* science. As we have said, Woolgar's notion of the RVS refers to a discourse that is used only in certain contexts, such as when one wants to claim authority so as to defend or legitimize an argument in cultures where the discourse of science is persuasive. This is precisely what Crowther and Hosking (2005) argued in their analysis of foot and mouth disease—'If "official government" scientists say we must cull, it must be true!'

Reflection

- *In what contexts are you most likely to use the discourse of science to defend, justify, or persuade?*
- *How would social life be different if the RVS were acknowledged as one of many available discourses?*

SHIFTING LOCAL DISCOURSES

Does the RVS capture the one way that science is and always was? Well, Woolgar and others (Latour and Woolgar 1979) argue that it does not seem to bear much resemblance to accounts emerging from ethnographic studies of what scientists *do* when they are in the process of "doing science" (Woolgar 1996). In addition, it is important to appreciate that science has varied considerably through the course of history. For example, there was a time when it was thought capable of producing facts that could *positively prove* the truth of some knowledge claim (positivism). This view gave way to post-positivism—a view that features the hypothetico-deductive approach (Gergen 1994; Kerlinger 1964), *falsification*, and probable truths rather than verification and the language of proof and certainty.[1]

Shifting constructions of science were perhaps most famously discussed in Thomas Kuhn's (1970) work, *The Structure of Scientific Revolutions*. Since then, differing constructions (or meta-theories) have been actively explored in some social science communities, such as organization studies (Chia 2003; Hassard 1991; Hosking 2011; Lewis and Keleman 2002; Schultz and Hatch 1996) and qualitative inquiry (Cunliffe 2010; Mir and Mir 2002) but not, for example, leadership (Hosking 2006; Uhl-Bien 2006). Kuhn wrote of "paradigms" as "coherent traditions of scientific research" (10), such as Copernican astronomy or Newtonian dynamics. He suggested, "Men whose research is based on shared paradigms are committed to the same rules and standards for scientific practice" (11).

He went on to argue that a paradigm is much more than shared rules and standards. It is reflected, for example, in decisions to use certain sorts of apparatus, measuring devices, or tools in particular ways (59); in decisions to follow particular procedures, applications, laws, and theories; and in *shared commitments to particular philosophical "fundamentals"* (Latour 1987). *Identification with a particular "tradition" or set of shared fundamentals is effectively a matter of becoming a member of a particular professional community* (Kuhn 1970). This is why we keep referring to community-based norms, values, and interests. For example, a tradition that claims that our health is dependent on our faith would entail very particular forms of practice. These practices would be quite different from a tradition that claims health as a byproduct of environment, bodily function, chemistry, and so forth. When health is viewed as a matter of faith, the tools for examining and improving one's health might include prayer, some sort of sacrificial offering to a greater being, penance for wrongdoing, and so forth. The diagnostic tools of modern Western medicine would have no place in this faith-based paradigm.

Kuhn focused on historical shifts in the particular "research tradition" or "paradigm" that is generally regarded as "normal science." Kuhn's account tended to emphasize one generally agreed-on set of community-based practices giving way to another that becomes the new normal science, so to speak. However, it seems that since he wrote his text, things have again moved on. The human sciences, depending on which community you look at, are no longer characterized by one generally agreed-on paradigm but by a variety that exist simultaneously. For example, Guba and Lincoln (1994) identified four paradigms and viewed them as "competing."

Writing a little later, Alvesson and Deetz (2000) identified four "social science perspectives" but presented them as "alternatives." This latter view suggests *relational constructionism be viewed as one possible community-based paradigm or meta-theory.* In the next section we will use Woolgar's features of the RVS to help us elevate dominant meta-theoretical assumptions and to introduce other possibilities relevant to our relational constructionist discourse.

META-THEORETICAL ASSUMPTIONS

Assumptions About the Human Actor

We have seen that the RVS embraces some crucial assumptions about scientists or, more generally, human actors—assumptions that could be otherwise. According to Woolgar, the RVS implicitly tells the story of the scientist as a relatively bounded being, possessing both a knowing mind and the capacity for autonomous action (agency). More precisely, the scientist is described as a "cognizing individual" who theorizes, conducts scientific procedures, observes, analyzes and interprets data, possesses knowledge, and so forth. In presenting this story, the RVS says absolutely nothing about the scientist as a community participant and makes no reference to the community (in this case, scientific) that Kuhn suggested creates, agrees, and maintains such constructions; an individualist discourse dominates.

The assumption of the cognizing, knowing individual does not match up well to the theories and findings of modern Western psychology and cognitive science. For example, early in the 20th century, psychology shifted from talk of sensation and sense *taking* to perception and constructive acts of sense *making*. It became widely accepted that any simple-minded empiricism that assumes we directly connect to a world of particulars as brute facts is deeply flawed. As Kuhn himself remarked, "fact and theory, discovery and invention, are not categorically and permanently distinct" (66)—which means that pure observation is impossible. Instead, it seems that observations are influenced, for example, by observers' theories and expectations, by the questions they ask, and by the tools and procedures they employ. "The operations and measurements that a scientist undertakes in the laboratory are not 'the given' of experience but rather are the 'collected with difficulty' " (Kuhn 1970, 136). And, we might add, part of the difficulty is that members of different communities select and organize observations in ways that reflect their own, partial community-based perspective—as we regularly see in the group exercise we outlined earlier.

Moving on from "simple-minded empiricism" or what some call "positivism" (Bentz and Shapiro 1998) brings us to the post-positivist discourse of science that holds that scientists *construct knowledge* by combining what is in the mind with what is in the world, so to speak. So, post-positivism collapses the dualist opposition of empiricism (knowledge reflects pure observations) and rationalism (knowledge is produced by a mind that can reason from general axioms to hidden laws and structures) and accepts that social-cultural factors influence knowledge. However, as its name suggests, post-positivism *revises* but does not radically change positivist assumptions. So, the singular and independently existing real world continues to be the focus of scientific interest in generalizable and cumulative knowledge. In this meta-theory, historical and cultural factors can be embraced but as factors that render scientific knowledge less than fully objective and less than completely certain. For history and culture to have a more major role—in the discourses of person, of construction, and of science—the root metaphor of mechanism and its assumption of independently existing objects, subject-object relations, and transcendental knowledge (of objects) has to change. In addition, the discourse of construction has to change to include science itself as a local-cultural, historically contingent, and relational process.

Assumptions About Discovering and Knowing Objects

On the issue of discovery, Woolgar suggests that the RVS presents discovery as a relatively simple, unequivocal act performed by a bounded, cognizing individual. Scientific methodology is spoken of as one that provides the cognizing agent with the tools for discovery. But are there other possibilities? Well, for a start, talk of discovery only makes the sense it does in relation to the particularities of the wider cluster of interrelated distinctions that characterize the RVS. Scientific methodology can only discover what the wider discourse assumes exists, which, in the case of the RVS, consists of independent and observable objects. More generally, it seems that we can only discover what fits within our social science perspective and is responsive to the questions we ask. The questions we form and the methods we design both facilitate and limit what we can know.

Again, Woolgar offers some pertinent reflections, this time in his deconstruction of the assumption of the 'given-ness' of experience. He does so by speaking of the assumption of independently existing objects as "the rhetoric of ontology" and links it with "the ideology of representation" (16). He describes the latter as

> The set of beliefs and practices stemming from the idea that various entities (meanings, motives, things, essences, reality, underlying patterns, cause, what is signified, intention, meaning, facts, objects and so on) underlie or pre-exist their surface representations (documents, appearances, signs, images, actions, behavior, language, knowledge and so on). (16)

And now what about knowledge and the way it is talked about in relation to the assumption of objects? Two related but distinct *epistemological positions* are associated with the assumption of objects and representations. The first Woolgar referred to as an epistemology of "naïve reflection." It assumes, for example, that conceptual language derives more or less straightforwardly from (i.e., "reflects") observations of the self-existing object—the underlying reality. So, for example, numbers, words, and pictures may represent real-world objects and their characteristics.

If we follow Kuhn's line of argument, then we must see observations as community-based constructions. More generally, "observations" are not "just" about independently existing objects in the world but reflect, for example, the paradigm, methods, questions, procedures, and interests that led to their production—or we could say—construction. This brings us to the second epistemological position, referred to by Woolgar as the "mediative view" and referred to by Guba and Lincoln as "critical realism"—where "critical" means 'not naïve.' Now a realist ontology continues to be centered but representations are viewed as necessarily imperfect. This view, which includes post-positivism, continues to assume a self-existing, cognizing agent who can act to discover and know (although never perfectly) some self-existing other and does so in some more or less blurred subject-object relation. This construction is found not only in discourses of science (meta-theories) but also in 'scientific' theories of, for example, leadership and change (Hosking 2004).

Reflection

- *What or who do you need to be you—what/who makes your identity or self?*
- *Where/when/how does this self begin and end?*
- *Do you feel differently about the person you are when someone close to you dies?*
- *When are you most you?*
- *Do your answers refer to other(s)? If so, what does this imply about the self-existing nature of you?*

Assumptions About Self, Other, and Relations: Subject-Object Constructions

The construction of the self (e.g., as a scientist) and other (e.g., as a separate and knowable object) has been spoken of both as "hard differentiation" (Berman 1981, 1990; Hollis 1994) and as a "subject-object" (S-O) discourse of self, other, and relations (Dachler and Hosking 1995; Fine 1994; Harding 1986). Of course, softer, non-subject-object constructions are also implied as possible. We will turn to this later. First, we need to summarize what "subject-object" means in this case; more detailed discussions can be found elsewhere (Hosking 2006, 2007a).

First, and by definition, an *active-passive binary* is reflected in talk of an active and responsible agent who relates to other(s) as a passive and available object on which to be acted. This construction is central to the empiricist, hypothesis-testing approaches we outlined earlier. It is central to approaches in which the scientist is active and acts toward other as available to be known (through research) and influenced (rationally—on the basis of empirical findings).[2]

Second is the assumption of bounded entities and entity characteristics. The latter are assumed to be outside processes to provide (relatively static) inputs to processes and perhaps to be affected by outcomes. For example, organizations are assumed to have structural and strategic characteristics (as inputs to organizational and inter-organizational processes) that can be manipulated to match the (assumed) characteristics of the organizational environment to produce certain levels of organizational effectiveness—theorized as the outcome of this relationship.

Third, the subject, and only the subject, is presented as active. One area of activity is clearly knowledge production. The subject is described as one who actively builds his or her own individual *knowledge that* other—IS this or that, possesses certain characteristics, needs to be changed, and so on. The scientist, as subject, builds positive knowledge or knowledge of probable relations between entities. This knowledge is (intended to be) *objective* rather than subjective. Objective knowledge, remember, is about other; it is free from idiosyncratic biases contributed by the knower or by the particular tools and procedures used; it is about 'other'—as known by the scientist (leader, change agent, etc.).[3]

Fourth, subjects are assumed actively to use their knowledge to achieve *"power over"* other as object. Power is presented as if it has rational foundations in, for example, the subject's knowledge of what other is, has, or does. Again, this theme appears in the discourse of science and in more local theories. For example, scientists are presented as those who may use their knowledge to design and manipulate the inquiry process (methodology), leading to their ability to predict and control, intervene and evaluate.[4]

Fifth, relations are reduced to instrumentalities as defined by and for the knowing subject. In subject-object relations, it is the subject who can know and who can rationally influence other; the subject's community-based rationality dominates. Other is an instrument for the subject's pursuit of the supposedly rational and value-free purposes of constructing generalizable knowledge that is free from individual bias. For example, scientific knowledge may support prediction and control and may contribute to progressively better ways of doing things. Furthering science and its production of generalizable knowledge is the science community's main objective.

Reflection

This active-passive dichotomy is very common. Can you see it in the following?

- *Theories of leadership?*
- *Constructions of gender and gender relations?*
- *Methodologies of organizational and community change?*
- *Your own inquiry/change work practices?*

Assumptions About Self, Other, and Relations: Blurring Subject-Object Constructions

Post-positivist science communities (1) accept that it is not possible to know whether or not we know the world as it really is because, for example, we can never have unmediated access to the real world; (2) accept that fully objective knowledge is unattainable; and (3) accept a revised notion of truth, for example, as that which is useful (Guba and Lincoln 1994). You could say post-positivists subscribe to a blurred epistemology that recognizes the ways in which individual acts of construction blur what is known of reality.

This said, it is harder to see much blurring of S-O in assumptions about what exists or in methodological practices. Subject-object dualism remains a "regulatory ideal" (Guba and Lincoln 1994, 110) in that knowing scientists must strive to be as separate as possible from the object(s) of their inquiry. The job of methodology continues to be the production of knowledge about (that assumed to be independently existing) 'real' reality. The scientist's focus continues to be on relatively objective knowledge and on knowledge accepted (at least by a scientific community) as "justified true belief" (Hollis 1994, 9). In sum, while many dualist assumptions are blurred, *they certainly are not abandoned* (Bem and De Jong 2006; Benton and Craib 2001).

Similar sorts of things could be said about many theories of construction, social construction, or constructivism. So, for example, researchers working within each theory often aim to say something (objective) about people (as research objects) *constructing* their more or less (in)accurate knowledge of an independently existing world. Scientific constructs such as mind maps, schema, narratives, and discourses are conceptualized as characteristics of individual minds and mind operations.

In sum, post-positivist assumptions and (social) constructivist theories blur some (primarily epistemological) subject-object assumptions and continue to prescribe subject-object relations in the conduct of scientific inquiry. Dualist themes continue to center the bounded and self-existing individual human whose characteristics include a singular self (*I* think) with a knowing mind (I *think*) (Hermans, Kempen, and Van Loon 1992). The knowing and influencing individual continues to be described in terms of personal characteristics such as mind, motives, and personality and continues to be constructed as one who uses language to (mis)represent an independently existing reality. Construction is an individual act—as is relating.

We have summarized some of the main themes of our discussion in Table 2.1. We invite you to see this not as a positive assertion of truth, but as a potentially useful tool or game that can help you to think about and further clarify your own assumptions and inquiry interests. You need to have some clarity about how you see yourself in relation to your inquiry, what you want it to achieve, and how you will justify your actions and knowledge claims.

Reflection

- *Look at the schema below and have a go at filling in the column headed "your inquiry"—keep it safe.*
- *When you have read the rest of the book—do the exercise again.*

- *More generally, we suggest that you think of this exercise as a useful discipline—as part of your (inquiry) practice—rather than a 'one shot deal.'*

We have taken you through this rather detailed and lengthy journey because our discourse of relational construction requires not just a blurring but also a *radical* re-construction of subject-object relations and a *radical* shift in basic assumptions and related practices. We turn to these in the following chapter.

Table 2.1 Comparison of Assumptions

Assumptions About	The Received View of Science	Post-Positivism	Your inquiry
What exists (self as scientist as well as the focus of our inquiry)	Bounded entities and "their" characteristics as separate existences in self-other relations	A more nuanced view of the boundaries and characteristics of humans (& therefore, scientists)	
What we can know—scientifically—about what (we assume) exists	Individuals can discover/know about real world objects; This knowledge is 'knowledge that' (the world is . . .); There are certain truths (naive realism)	Knowledge can never be fully objective; "Justified true belief"—empirical data provide justifications for knowledge claims; There are probable, useful truths (critical realism)	
How we can produce that knowledge	Through individual acts of reasoning and deciding, and through the design and control of generally agreed methods, rules and procedures	Design and control of methodology, and methods of empirical inquiry; Still striving to achieve control and unbiased observations; Reflexive evaluation of how well we did so	
Self-Other Relations	Hard self-other differentiation in which the subject assumes to know and influence other, treated as a passive, knowable and formable object; Instrumental	The scientist strives for a methodology of hard subject-object differentiation—so as to produce (relatively) objective knowledge; Instrumental	

3 Our Community
Relational Constructionism

"a mad tea party"

MOVING TOWARD A RELATIONAL
DISCOURSE OF CONSTRUCTION

Until now we have discussed scientific practices and scientific theories together with philosophical matters that have a direct influence on science as a way of knowing. But, the meta-theories we have reviewed keep separate *"the context of discovery"* (defined as the province of science—or, put otherwise: what science *does*) and *"the context of justification"* (defined as the province of philosophy—or, put otherwise: the assumptions we reviewed in the last chapter). Separating these two contexts has the effect of protecting science from the dents that historical-cultural factors might otherwise make in what is referred to as scientific rationality, thereby allowing science to be seen as trans-historical and trans-cultural. The separation of discovery and justification demarcates and elevates science from other ways of knowing (that do not "count as" science) and from knowledge claims that are not grounded in a scientific methodology.

The community-based discourse that we now introduce—relational constructionism—is *not* founded on the assumption that the contexts of discovery and justification (science and analytic philosophy) are or should be distinct. Indeed, relational constructionist premises imply that this demarcation is (a) a community-based construction, by (b) a different community (post-positivist science), and (c) could be otherwise. Kuhn (1970), whose arguments about paradigms we mentioned earlier, offered an elegant account of the *social or relational* aspects of scientific communities. He made the important point that the normative standards by which discoveries are made are themselves a by-product of the rationale or rationality that characterizes that particular community or, using Wittgenstein's (1953) term, "form of life." Thus, distinctions between science and philosophy, between "discoveries in nature" and "rational justifications" are to be understood as local to a particular community and its particular historical moment. Some use the language of "modern" and "postmodern" to speak of different social science perspectives and their approaches to inquiry. As we will see, this connecting of community and construction is central to our version of relational constructionism.

MODERNISM, POSTMODERNISM, AND OUR DISCOURSE OF CONSTRUCTION

The terms modernism and postmodernism are used to mean many different things in different communities, and so we are hesitant about employing them here. However, we find it helpful to refer to our own discourse as "postmodern" (in a very particular sense) as a way of summarizing relational constructionism and differentiating it from other discourses of construction. We are able to do this because our colleagues Ken Gergen and Tojo Thatchenkery (1996) wrote about (post)modernism in ways that are directly relevant and helpful to our present purposes. They identified three themes associated with what they call the modernist view of science (see Table 3.1). The first is the assumption of individual rationality, the second is the emphasis on individual observation and empiricist philosophy, and the third is the view of language as representation—as "truth bearing." To these three we can add a fourth, the presence of entitative thinking (Hosking and Morley 1991) or an "ontology of being" (Chia 1995), and a fifth, an interest in producing objective knowledge about 'what it is' and 'what is (probably) real,' which we spoke about in the previous chapter.

Gergen and Thatchenkery's Modernist Themes

First is the assumption of *individual rationality*, which can be understood as growing out of particular cultural-historical processes that produced what was then considered to be a liberating shift away from the power of church and state. The Enlightenment, as this period in Western cultures and history is now known, challenged the authority of church and state by proposing that all persons, with careful observation and experience, could make informed and justifiable decisions. Thus, the idea that any individual had the ability to be rational and make wise choices significantly changed the way communities, cultures, and all social institutions operated. Decision making was removed from the hands of church and state and placed in the hands of ordinary citizens.

Second is the emphasis on *individual observation and empiricist philosophy*, which presumes that careful observation of one's self and the world will yield knowledge of what really is the case. This brings us to our third theme, which posits that when we describe reality, our descriptions (our words) can stand in for or represent what is real; we discussed this in the last chapter. Notice the very particular understanding of language

Table 3.1 Gergen and Thatchenkery's Sketch of Modernist Assumptions

Assumptions	Modernism
About rationality	Individual
How we know	Observation and empiricist philosophy
Language	Truth bearing

embedded in this view. *Language is assumed to represent reality.* Words and actions are assumed to stand in for real things in the world.[1]

To Gergen and Thatchenkery's three themes we add a fourth—a realist ontology. When we adopt a representational view of language (word describes object), we make objects (or entities) of ourselves and all that surrounds us. And, it can be difficult to challenge someone's conviction that a tree is an object that can be objectively observed. However, as we have mentioned, it is easier to challenge the construction of love, justice, freedom, and democracy as entities or characteristics of entities.

Reflection

- *How do we know justice when we see it?*
- *How can we be certain that the words we use to describe justice are accurate?*
- *Similarly, how can we know our own minds or the minds of others?*
- *Where is your mind and where does it stop?*

From a relational constructionist perspective, justice, love, freedom, and democracy (and trees!) are viewed as constructed in language-based, relational processes; entified constructions are just that—constructions.

Our fifth and last theme concerns the modernist focus on objective-subjective knowledge. We can easily see how these assumptions invite the belief that, with the right methods and careful observation and with the right experience, a person (an entity acting as a scientist) can claim, with some sufficient degree of objectivity, what is (probably) true. The idea of the cognizing individual is now so familiar to us, why would we want to challenge or change this discourse? Surely my cognitive abilities allow me to make choices. If my choices are poor then my individual competencies will be assessed as deficient (and some remedial work might be deemed in order). But Gergen and Thatchenkery's account of alternative, postmodern understandings of the person-world relationship shows that the modernist discourse just summarized is only one possible discourse.

Gergen and Thatchenkery's Postmodern Themes

Gergen and Thatchenkery (1996) introduce the very different constructions of rationality, empiricism, and language characteristic of what they
call postmodern thinking. They summarize three shifts. The first is a shift
from individual to communal rationality. Rationality is no longer seen as
a cognitive property of an individual but as a local-cultural performance.
To echo our earlier discussion of Kuhn, to be "rational" is to participate
in some local tradition, re-constructing one's own identity as a member of
a particular community as one does so. Rationality is a relational process.

The second shift that Gergen and Thatchenkery identify is a movement from empirical method to social construction. This shift reflects the
wide recognition that "our understanding of phenomena are [sic] themselves theory laden, as are the methods used in their illumination" (235).
There is a connection with the first theme; methods, concepts, and so
on make (non)sense in relation to some wider tradition (theory, perspective, or "intelligibility"). So, for example, the way we "do" inquiry (methods, procedures, analysis), the way we talk and write about it (using, for
example, the language of variables, observations, and data) both reflect a
particular tradition and are "constitutive" of it (Woolgar 1996).

Gergen and Thatchenkery's third theme concerns the different view of
language—not as representational—but as "social action" and as "world
constituting" (236). Just as we did earlier, Gergen and Thatchenkery call
on Wittgenstein's theory of "language games" that 'do' a particular "form
of life." "Language does not describe action but is itself a form of action"
(236). In this view, to 'do science' is to participate in particular community-based practices. Of specific relevance to our present discussions are
the science communities that subscribe to quite different "meta-theories"
in their different ways of doing their (own, local) rationality.

We want to emphasize that, for us, the issue is not whether modernism or postmodernism is right or wrong, better or worse. Indeed, in our
view, right/wrong, better/worse constructions, together with a logic of

Table 3.2   Gergen and Thatchenkery's Sketch of Modern and
Postmodern Assumptions

Assumptions	Modernism	Postmodernism
About rationality	Individual	Communal, local-cultural
How we know	Observation and empiricist philosophy	Social construction
Language	Truth bearing	Constitutive

either/or, are central to the modernist discourse. It is important to recognize that as postmodern work gets pulled into right/wrong debates, the already dominant discourse of modernism continues to be reproduced. We view modernism and postmodernism as *discursive resources*. We do not claim that either is true or false; we *do* claim that the way we orient ourselves to the world will be radically different depending on the discourse in use.

A postmodern focus (as defined here) includes not only changed assumptions but also changed questions and interests; as we often say, 'everything changes.' For us, a key issue concerns the kinds of realities that we are a part of and contribute to making, for example, in our (research) work. So what sort of world do we invite each other into when we act as if it is possible to represent the one way things really are? And, in contrast, what sort of world do we invite each other into when we assume realities are community-based local, historical, and cultural co-constructions? Both sorts of inquiry construct local-communal realities—but very different ones. One where there are experts and non-experts versus one where there are multiple and perhaps conflicting realms of expertise.

In our view, the postmodern themes we have outlined here do not simply say things in a different (and sometimes hard to understand) way about the 'same' (modernist) territory. Rather, these themes provide the possibility to engage others (theorists, practitioners, researchers, as well as all social actors) in activities that broaden our resources for social life. This is the approach taken by Newman and Holzman (1997) in their book, *The End of Knowing*. Their (postmodern) interest is not to have others learn or know about postmodernism as an abstract theory or 'thing.' Rather, their interest is in the very *practice* of postmodernism as it might open up different possibilities, as a *performance* that literally puts into action, and thus makes available, new relational resources. To this end, these postmodern themes and related inquiry practices could be said to constitute *another "territory"* (Korzybski 1933)—not just another map of a pre-existing (modernist) territory.

Table 3.3 A Different Territory

	Modernism	*Postmodernism*
Scientific interest	Finding out/discovering how things really (probably) are	Co-constructing local-cultural realities
Theory/practice	Development and testing of theories	Practice/performance; theory as practice

OUR POSTMODERN DISCOURSE OF
RELATIONAL CONSTRUCTIONISM

The themes that contribute to our particular discourse of relational constructionism appear in many different areas of practice and in many different literatures including feminist and other radical critiques of science, communication studies, cognitive and social psychology, sociology, family therapy, critical social anthropology (Danziger 1997; Gergen 1994; Hosking and Morley 2004), and some areas of postmodernism and post structuralism (Foucault 1980; Latour 1987). They are not new, and they manifest in different ways in different communities.

As we have said, our discourse of relational constructionism does not assume an individual mind that aims to know an external and independently existing reality. Instead, we center *processes of relating*, sometimes we say communicating, and view these as processes in which *relational realities* are constructed. These relational realities include constructions of what it is to be a person, of 'the world,' of (a particular) self in relation to (particular) others, of self-other boundary, of science, and so on. In other words, we are not talking about mind operations producing objective or subjective knowledge of reality. Nor are we proposing a relativist discourse by rejecting real-world assumptions and allowing that 'anything goes.' As we have said, this is another territory. It is a territory without the objective-subjective, real-relativist dualisms, which are local to a different (modernist) discourse community.

As we have said, when we write about relating or communicating, we are not assuming the existence of a bounded individual influencing, persuading, and making meaning. Rather, we are talking about ongoing, local-cultural, local-historical processes as they construct relational realities including, for example, the realities of a debate, of an ethnographic inquiry, of an interview, or indeed any practice that some community wants to call inquiry, community development, or organizational change work. Perhaps it is time to summarize some of the key themes of relational constructionism, and then we can discuss them in greater detail.

First, talk of the individual self, of private mental operations and of individual knowledge, gives way to *centering relational processes*—to what people do as participants in, and co-producers of, particular practice communities. Here, we focus on how our actions invite certain sorts of responses from others and how, in turn, the actions of others—where 'others' includes not just humans but also, for example, technology and ecology—invite particular ways of acting from us. It is to these ongoing processes of inter-action, of relating, that we turn our attention—what are *we* doing rather than what am *I* doing.

Second, instead of assuming self-existing entities and knowledge of the same, relational constructionism assumes and gives ontology to relational processes as they (re)construct local realities. In other words, it is the process of relating that is examined and not individuals and their private, individual properties (such as mind and motives). These relational realities are not 'mind stuff' but are made in words and deeds, so to speak. As we have said, Gergen and Thatchenkery speak of multiple "local rationalities" while, in a similar style of thinking, Wittgenstein (1953) spoke of multiple "language games" together with their related "forms of life." We are interested in how ways of acting and becoming in the world unfold in ongoing relational realities.

Third, the idea that an individual possesses a self gives way to a processual and relational conception of multiple self-other relations in ongoing construction in relational processes. Thus, the notion of a stable and unified self is now seen as an accomplishment of joint action rather than "proof" of a true, inner self. Fourth, subject-object relations are no longer assumed to be how things really are or how they should be. Relational processes *may construct* hard self-other differentiation in subject-object relations. This probably remains the most common way of conducting research. But how may/do we construct softer self-other differentiation? Perhaps we might draw on something similar to what Buber (cited in Buber, Friedman, and Smith 1965) calls moving I-It relations to I-Thou (instead of I-It) relations.

Fifth, relational processes are the locus of both stability and change; they close down and open up possibilities. Thus, inquiry, when viewed as a relational process, may do more or less to open up possible selves and worlds.

Let us summarize the themes that define our "territory" or landscape:

- *Not* individual self and private interiority, *but* relational processes;
- *Not* self-existing entities and knowledge of the same, *but* relational processes making multiple local rationalities;
- *Not* a unified, singular self, *but* multiple self-other relations in ongoing construction;
- *Not* inevitably subject-object relations ("hard" self-other differentiation), *but* soft self-other differentiation as a possibility;
- *Not* change from one stable state to another, *but* processes that close down and open up possibilities.

DEVELOPING THE REFRAIN OF RELATIONAL PROCESSES

We can now thicken our talk of relational processes. We will present them as (a) inter-actions, that are (b) multiple and often simultaneous and (c) local in both a cultural and historical sense.

Inter-actions

As we sketched above, talk of the individual as having a self and as possessing a mind and individual knowledge gives way to discourses of relational processes viewed broadly as inter-actions or communication. This, of course, raises the question of how inter-actions are understood. Many constructionist writings give language a central role as the medium in which representing (as constructing) 'goes on.' This emphasis on language shifts attention away from the dualistic distinctions and characterizations that (apparently) describe an external world with properties, humans with senses and the ability to collect data, internal mind operations that process data, and sender-receiver, information exchange models of communication.

A variety of tools have been used for talking about relational processes. Some emphasize written and spoken language as the media in which construction goes on through terms such as storytelling, conversation, narrative, and discourse. Sometimes the term performance is used, perhaps, to give more emphasis to non-linguistic actions and/or to construction as practice rather than mind stuff (Newman and Holzman 1997). Similarly, some writers employ the term "actant"—and write of networks of relations among actants—which seems neatly to avoid suggesting that relating goes on only between persons. For example, Latour (1987) speaks of an actant as "whoever and whatever is represented" (84), including people, objects, statements, facts, events, and so forth, and spoke of "the enrolling and controlling processes" that help to construct and stabilize realities. Broadly speaking, we are using the term inter-action (a) to signal a performance (b) that involves a coming together (c) of "whoever and whatever" that (re) constructs person-world relations as (d) relational realities.

This postmodern discourse of construction stands apart from modernist, constructi*vist* discourses in a number of important ways. First, it makes it clear that both human and non-human actors contribute to, and are products of, reality construction processes. Second, reality construction is described as a process of inter-action—of relations between actants— and not individual action. Third, it is talk about the "textuality" of *all* relational realities (Stenner and Eccleston 1994) and not just written and spoken texts. Last, science is included in the discourse. In other words, science is treated as a community of practice that, like other communities, is (re)constructed in inter-actions (Latour and Woolgar 1979). This brings us to our next theme—the simultaneous multiplicity of inter-actions.

Multiple, Simultaneous Inter-actions

Modernism sharply distinguishes human actors and natural and man-made objects such that language and scientific interest is presumed as (relatively) objective knowledge about other. For example, in Magritte's painting *Ceci n'est pas une pipe*, the painter, the painting, the viewer, and other possibly relevant contexts are treated as independent entities, whereas complex, ongoing, relational processes are turned into a seemingly singular and stable It (e.g., the painting) in relation to the Aristotelian logic of either-or (it is either a pipe or it is not).

In contrast, relational constructionism opens up what Bruno Latour (1987) called the "black box" of relating. It does so by centering multiple, simultaneous inter-actions (rather than a singular object); by centering the production, performance, or 'the how' of ongoing processes (rather than 'the what' of inputs and/or outputs); and by remaining open to the possibility of multiple and changing constructions as 'content.' Relational constructionism assumes that many simultaneous inter-actions continuously contribute to the processes of constructing reality. So, for example, in the case of Magritte's painting, these could include relating the visual symbol (which many would say is a picture of a pipe) with the written text below it (which says *Ceci n'est pas une pipe*), the written text with the French language, the written text with the Dutch language (!), narratives of earlier viewings, of what others have said about the painting, of what counts as a painting, of what is appropriately called a pipe, and so on.

So, the question 'What is it?' could invite many equally correct answers: It is a pipe, it is a painting of a pipe, it is a paradox, it is a work of art. Our interest is not in 'What is it?' questions, nor in assumed entities; our interest is in how ongoing relational processes construct and re-construct local ontologies as forms of life.

Local-cultural, Local-historical Constructions

In relational constructionism, relating is considered to be both ongoing and to construct stabilizing effects. The latter could include social conventions, musical forms, science, organizational and societal structures, Western psychology, what some might call nature, facts, or artifacts, and multiple self-other constructions. But not all inter-actions become stabilized; some go unheard, unseen, unnoticed. The fate of an identity claim (this is/is not a pipe) depends on whether or not it is warranted as "real and good" (Gergen 1994). We are not free to simply claim what is or is not the case without responsive support. Or, as Latour (1987) would have it, the fate of a statement depends on others who have to read it, take it up, and use it—others have to be "enrolled" and they have to be "controlled."

Some cultures (as forms of life) are able to enroll and control on a larger scale than others—and so may appear, for example, to have more powerful Gods or better methods for producing objective knowledge. Once a particular performance becomes stabilized, for example, a greeting convention, a particular sonata form, or what counts as middle C, other possibilities may find it harder to achieve warrant. As Beethoven discovered at a premiere of one of his sonatas, it may be harder to enroll and control an audience when its participants are sure they already know what is real and good (in this case, what was and what was not a sonata). As we have already indicated, such difficulties are especially likely to be encountered when discourses of right and wrong have already been stabilized (Alvesson and Deetz 2000).

Our reference to *local* processes should be understood in contrasting relation to narratives of *general* knowledge—knowledge that is trans-cultural and trans-historical. Relational constructionism emphasizes that what is warranted or discredited is local to the ongoing practices that (re) construct a particular culture (e.g., the sonata form in Western and not Japanese music). But we should also emphasize that inter-actions vary in the scale of their inter-connections. This means that 'local' could be as broad as Western or post-Enlightenment. The locals (by which we also mean scientists) may take it for granted that their particular constructions are universal, (probably) transcendental truths. However, the present line of argument suggests the essential artfulness of stabilized effects and draws attention to the relational processes that make and re-make them.

Our talk of 'local' includes cultural and historical aspects. However, our reference to history is not intended as a reference to temporary truths when transcendental truths are potentially available. Nor is it intended to imply a linear and unidirectional process in which the present is a moment between (the now finished) past and the (yet to come) future. Such a view of process goes together with the separation of means and ends, process and content, "tool and result" (Vygotsky 1978) and reproduces a very particular con-struction of time.

Rather, we say that relational processes have a historical quality in the sense that acts always supplement prior acts or texts and have implications for how the process will go on. The ongoing present reproduces some previ-ous structurings, for example, the convention of shaking hands, and acts in relation to possible and probable futures (e.g., that a greeting will be success-fully performed). In other words, all acts (sometimes we say texts) supple-ment other acts (contexts) *and* are available for possible supplementation and possible (dis)crediting. In the discourse of constructionism, inter-actions, and particularly regularly repeated ones, "make history," so to speak, and history is constantly being re-made (Hora as cited in Hermans, Kempen, and Van Loon 1992; Vico as cited in Hermans, Kempen, and Van Loon 1992).

Put very simply, we talk about the local-cultural-historical aspects of realities as follows. People coordinate their activities with (what they may language as) other people, things, landscapes, and so forth. From these inter-actions, patterns emerge. Think of how quickly you and your col-leagues take your seats at a staff meeting and continue the pattern in subsequent meetings. Patterns generate standards and expectations that participants use to assess their own actions and the actions of others. So, for example, if someone takes your usual seat you may be surprised and taken aback—"Who told *him* that seat was available?" These evaluating and standardizing practices get carried into future interactions, where they will be confirmed and sustained, challenged, or transformed. Thus, from the very simple process of coordinating we develop local-cultural norms and values and patterns of influence that, in turn, serve as "common sense" justification for future coordinations.

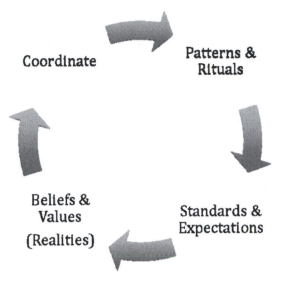

Figure 3.1 The process of constructing relational/communal realities.

Relational Realities

We have said that multiple, simultaneous, ongoing forms of relating (re) construct relational realities. In this view, the individual is not the agent of reality construction. In this view, identity (and other assumed entity characteristics such as personality, organizational goals and structures, etc.) is not singular and fixed and does not function as the necessary defining characteristic of someone or something. Rather identity and the assumed characteristics of entities are theorized (a) as byproducts of relational interchange and so (b) multiple and variable (different realities in different self-other relations), and (c) as performed rather than possessed in local-cultural-historical networks of ongoing forms of relating. In other words, relational processes are "reality-constituting practice(s)" (Edwards and Potter 1992, 27). Relational processes (re)construct science, scientists, scientific inquiry, and what is not science; they construct markets, nature, technology, and self-other as relational realities.

The concept of dialogue is often used to explore language-based relational processes and relational realities. Bakhtin (1981) describes dialogue as a *responsive* activity. According to Wood (2004), Bakhtin takes the view that "it is not enough to say that response is central to dialogue. Response—or, more precisely, responsiveness—arises out of and is made possible by qualities of thought and talk that allow transformation in how one understands the self, others, and the world they inhabit" (xvi). Bakhtin (1981), Sampson (1993), and others describe the Western individualistic construction of person as monological. Monologue refers to the self-serving, I-It (Buber, Friedman, and Smith 1965) forms of relations generated within modernist discourse. In contrast, a dialogical view offers a very different understanding of humans and inter-action. As Sampson (1993) says, *"the most important thing about people is not what is contained within them, but what transpires between them"* (20).[2] Further, he goes on to say that the "emphasis (is) on the idea that people's lives are characterized by the ongoing conversations and dialogues they carry out in the course of their everyday activities" (20).

Returning to the start of this chapter, we can clearly see that, in a relational constructionist view, the "context of discovery" and "context of justification" are not separated. What we are able to know, the relational realities we construct and inhabit, depends on our engagements with other, as does our ability to offer what others accept as a coherent or rational justification.

SOCIAL CONSTRUCTION AS PRACTICAL THEORY

Let us conclude this chapter by noting the important point that *relational constructionism invites us to direct our attention to the realities and relations constructed in the practice of any inquiry*, including attention to the questions asked, the methods used, and the methodology followed. We can illustrate this with another story from one of our students:

> I am a member of the Police force. I have noticed that our information systems are hardly ever evaluated. This is puzzling me because development, maintenance, and evolution of such large-scale systems involve a lot of public resources. For my Ph.D., I would like to investigate how such systems could be evaluated because evaluation can provide key information to improve (police) organizations. The dominant approach to information system evaluation reflects the modernist paradigm. Rather than refine the techniques and concepts of this paradigm, I believe that a dialogue between modern and postmodern paradigms is an interesting (and new) way to conduct evaluation (Schultz and Hatch 1996). Some suggest that evaluative claims constructed from either a modern or a postmodern perspective are just different (Abma 2000, 7). But are they and, if so, in what ways?
>
> The above provokes the following research question: *What are the contrasts and connections between the claims constructed by a systematic-modern and affirmative-postmodern information system evaluation, and what are the appreciations of decision makers regarding the constructed claims?* In this study I intend to start a dialogue between paradigms.
>
> I will evaluate at least one information system in both a modern and postmodern way. Subsequently, from both empirical evaluations,

differences and similarities will be explored. My research question will be addressed by combining this with an additional study of decision makers' appreciations of the knowledge claims constructed in both evaluations.

This practitioner showed that he understood that different "paradigms" would generate very different practicalities—not better or worse in any absolute sense—but different. We have tried to sketch a relational constructionism that does not try to eliminate or demonize other traditions and that orients toward possibilities and resources. Relational constructionism urges us to attend to the traditions, the communities, the situated practices, and the local understandings implicit in what becomes real and good. Whereas modernist theory and practice aim to solve problems, cure illness, and achieve social, environmental, and scientific advancements, relational constructionism aims to explore the sorts of life that become possible through different inter-actions, including (but not restricted to) different ways of talking. The metaphor of performance can be useful, for example, because it lets go of the focus on methods as ways of producing knowledge and instead directs attention to the ways relational realities are created. As we relate in some more or less transformative inquiry process, who we are and who or what is other are co-created together with an order of value. We create—we perform together with others, with props, costumes, and so on—a world, a life, and a lived reality (Gergen 2009b).

If relational realities arise out of relational engagement (conversations, performances, dialogues), then we must pause and reflect, we must ask in what other ways we might talk about or perform this topic, this issue, this problem. We do not have to inquire or write as if the world is, or should be, just one way. Rather, our inquiries could open up new possible ways of being human and new possible ways of "going on together" (Wittgenstein 1953)—the topic of our next chapter.

4 Inquiry as Engaged Unfolding

"when I find a thing . . . it's generally a frog or a worm"

THE QUESTION OF METHOD

Something that comes up time and again in our workshops is the question of method. We are often asked: "What method should I use?" "Is this a constructionist method?" We have found that many people assume, for example, that discourse analysis is a relational constructionist method (because it focuses on language). And they think that using a questionnaire is not (because it deals with numbers or categorical responses). There are a number of important points to make here. The first is that there is no such thing as a relational constructionist method. Relational constructionism is a meta-theory or discourse of (human) science. It provides *a general orientation* toward all relational processes, including those that might be called inquiry, intervention or development, leadership or organizing. This general orientation invites us to view all activities in which humans participate, all inquiry and theorizing—including relational constructionism—as a relational process. In principle this means that we could use anything that positive science would call a method, including, for example, statistics, experiments, and surveys.

Our second point follows from the argument that methods have no meaning in and of themselves. As we said in the conclusion to the last chapter, how we think about, use, talk, and write about methods activates a particular meta-theory or discourse of science. In other words, methods are neither free standing, nor are they necessarily attached to any one particular discourse. What becomes central for the constructionist is *how we practice any particular 'method'* or, more generally, how we 'do' our inquiry. For us, relational constructionist assumptions guide the questions we ask, how we try to answer them, what we count as a fact, what we recognize as rigor, the language tools we employ—indeed, all aspects of inquiry.

To illustrate this, let us further consider how 'method' is understood in the context of post-positivist inquiry. 'Method talk' is usually associated with relatively fixed notions of procedure where the latter can be evaluated. If you have ever tried to analyze large amounts of written text, such as interview transcripts, you might recall your attempts to find rules of method that you could follow. We feel safe in guessing that you did not find them. Speaking more generally, we can say that the possibility of method—of being able to specify ahead of time what to do, how, and so on—very much depends on how much you can and want to simplify and control your inquiry. Regardless of your meta-theory, a considerable amount of "craft work" (Silverman 2010) is always required. So if you are thinking you will 'use' some sort of interview, ethnography, document analysis, or whatever, you will have to work out how to use it in relation to your meta-theoretical assumptions, your research purposes, and so on.

This brings us back to relational constructionism: In what sorts of relational realities do you want to participate? Do you want to feature and elevate the practices, values, and interests of positive science, for example, or would you prefer to give more space to other (non-science) communities and their ways of doing things? What do the local communities participating in the inquiry process want? Any inquiry is likely to involve multiple community-based rationalities and interests, so it will be necessary to consider at what point and how they might enter into the conversation.

This brings us to our third point, which is that the issue of 'method' or form is not necessarily one for (only) you, in relation to (just) your science community, to decide and not necessarily one that can be decided ahead of time. Some decisions obviously must be made in advance. Yet, these decisions also are made within a relational context. Your choice to examine a particular issue, topic, or situation emerges in the context of our own community-based participations. This brings us back to your inquiry as a process that (re)creates particular realities and relations. If you feel attracted to relational constructionism, you may well want to depart from ways of relating that construct your self as the knowing inquirer and other as available for you to know and influence; this is what we earlier called subject-object relations. If so, you will probably want to be sensitive to other—to other local-cultural rationalities or communities who are in some way implicated in your inquiry. Additionally, you might want to be sensitive to place, to local language games, and to forms of communication such as talk or e-mails, dance, poetry, and so on. The following case illustrates this.

Dian Marie was the Ph.D. advisor for a development worker in the Philippines. Shayamal is a native Bangladeshi; he spoke none of the languages of the communities in which he was working. Many of the locals could not read or write, and his non-governmental organization (NGO) wanted him to use questionnaires and to produce statistical summaries of his findings. Dian Marie encouraged him instead to use a storytelling approach, inviting the locals to tell their stories in the ways they wanted to tell them. They did so, not only in words but also in dance and drawing. Of course in writing his thesis, he had to work with the forms and language of yet another community (academia). The 'hows and whys' of any inquiry will be many and varied depending on the particular communities involved. The more relationally sensitive and engaged you want to be, the more you will want to leave open the space for multiple community-based voices to influence the what, how, why, or who for.

Our fourth point follows from this. If you wish to be relationally responsive, in the moment, as the inquiry progresses, this is likely to lead you to lean away from design and methods. Most likely relational responsiveness will require a great deal of talk, conversation, and dialogue. *Often you will not be directly involved* in these conversations. You let go of control or rather the illusion of control. You will attempt to craft a process that opens up to multiplicity, to ongoing-developing-changing realities and relations, to other(ness)—including possible changes in self and in your positions on particular issues. You will probably lean toward ways of working that make space for thick textured descriptions rather than statistics (although this is not necessarily the case). Indeed, you may well find yourself drawn toward approaches that use the language of narrative or storytelling, discourse, or ethnography.

Giving space for inquiry processes to unfold in these ways may mean that your relations with particular practice communities may vary considerably during the course of your inquiry (Ceglowski 2001). Returning to the earlier example, Shayamal had to find ways to be responsive to his employer, to the communities in which he was working, and to the scientific/academic community in which his thesis would be evaluated. These differing relations came in and out of prominence at different points in the inquiry process and were played out in different relational forms or media. For example, the thesis for the scientific/academic community required a written form, but Shayamal's inter-actions with the villagers in remote mountain settings involved other forms such as talk, listening, playing, and living together (Saha 2009).

Last, we should again emphasize that relational processes go on in many forms other than conceptual language. However, as soon as we think, talk, and write about relational processes, conceptual language is necessarily implicated. It would be a pity if we forgot that relating is embodied and includes the construction and use of artifacts together with other bodies, sentient or not. Relating is much more than 'just' conceptual language; it is live and ongoing (Shotter 2010). It might be good to retain considerable humility over what is possible once we talk and write about 'it.'

Let's summarize our discussion (so far) on method:

- There is less of a concern about method (as in finding the 'right' one) and more of a *general orientation* toward all human activities;
- What is important is how we craft our 'methods'—given our meta-theory—in all aspects of our inquiry;
- One issue is that of how we can give space to multiple, local, community-based rationalities;
- One distinctive possibility is to look for ways to practice relationally responsive inquiry (McNamee and Gergen 1999); and

- Because relating is much more than conceptual language, we want to explore how to give space to this.

Perhaps we have reached the point where an overview of some key orientations implied or opened up by our relational constructionist approach to inquiry would be useful.

KEY RELATIONAL CONSTRUCTIONIST ORIENTATIONS

Key to everything is our assumption of the co-constructed nature of relational realities. Just as methods are community-based, they are also co-constructed performances with members of particular communities. To that end, the unfolding nature of our performances together becomes central. When we position ourselves as inquirers, we have ideas about what and who and where and how we want to focus our inquiry. Yet, as a constructionist inquirer, that original positioning is always open to amendment. Using the language of Alvesson and Deetz (2000), our positioning would be "local-emergent" rather than "elite, a priori." Rather than work with design and method, we prefer minimal structures and improvisation. Of course, some important decisions must be made before we embark on any inquiry. Yet, as we mentioned earlier, even these emerge within particular relational communities and then are more or less open to crediting or discrediting by those with whom we conduct our inquiry.

Further, we start with the assumption that multiple practice communities or stakeholders participate in our inquiry. In other words, we do not center the "consensus" assumption (Alvesson and Deetz 2000) of one single external reality and descriptions of the same, but rather we orient toward multiplicity, fragmentation, or what Alvesson and Deetz called "dissensus." For us, the challenge is to give space to these multiple local rationalities and let them be. In addition, we might want to lean toward opening up rather than closing down possibilities, a move that is distinctly different from the proclivities of positive science.

Also important are the many local and practical concerns of those who participate in the inquiry. Not all inquiry interests need be oriented toward the production of new knowledge or new solutions to societal problems. We will pause for a moment and give you some space to think through some possibilities.

Reflection

- *How might an organization or community struck by AIDS use inquiry to create new ways of working and living together?*
- *How might a study of leadership facilitate ways of leading that make space for collaborative relations among multiple, different local rationalities?*

- *How could a community development worker give space to multiple local rationalities rather than imposing science-based norms and values?*

In the remainder of this chapter, we hope to give you some help in thinking about possibilities. We will focus on narrative or storytelling, discourse and discourse analysis, interviewing, and ethnography. We will concentrate on how you might think about and work with these approaches, paying particular attention to how this would differ from a positive science approach.

Narrative or Storytelling

Given our relational constructionist discourse, all inquiry—whether an experiment, a survey, or an interview—can be viewed as narrative or storytelling/making. According to Foster and Bochner (2008), inquiry embraces "the details of lived experience, the reflexive relationship between personal interaction and cultural contexts, and the dialogic and dialectical complexity of relationships and communities" (92). As we said earlier, the inquirer is literally engaged in the process of *making* self an inquirer in relation to particular others (Howard 1991) as well as in relation to narratives of science, professional practice, organization development, and so on.

The explicit use of the language of narrative or storytelling has become increasingly popular in communities such as psychology (Sarbin 1986), organizational studies (Boje 1995; Calas and Smircich 1991; Czarniawska 2001), and therapy (White and Epston 1990). Work of this sort can include narrative interviews and narrative analysis of interviews. It also includes different sorts of narrative analysis of written and spoken texts, including documents, archival materials, e-mails, telephone calls, films, and magazines—the possibilities are endless. However, we must remind you of what we said earlier about 'method.' Methods are neither freestanding nor tied to a particular meta-theory. Just because the language of narrative or storytelling is used should not be taken to imply that the meta-theory is necessarily postmodern, relational constructionist. Indeed, narrative approaches are often employed within a post-positivist perspective.

Modernist approaches to narrative assume that they have a beginning, middle, and end and perhaps other structural characteristics (thus, not all text is narrative). In addition, identified narratives are treated as individual (rather than relational) texts to be collected, made sense of, and spoken about by the expert researcher/scientist. Parker (2005) warns that, in a positive science approach, narrative analysis is presented as if the researcher has captured the story of the research participants. He further warns that analysis proceeds as if the narrative serves as a "good example" of what this issue/topic is about, and as if there is one (probably) correct interpretation. The relational constructionist differs from the positive science approach in all these aspects. In the following, we focus on postmodern, relational constructionist forms of inquiry that utilize narrative.

As we set out earlier, we see actions or texts as more or less local and thus embedded in multiple inter-textual relations. This means that we view narratives as emerging within local rationalities and as co-constructions where the inquirer is part of, rather than apart from, the narrative. Our postmodern, relational constructionist purpose now may be thought of as articulating "local and practical concerns" (Gergen and Thatchenkery 1996). As we said in Chapter 3, this means articulating multiplicity and in this way giving voice to practices and possibilities that usually are muted, suppressed, or silenced. In this view, we see:

- Story construction as a process of creating reality, in which the self/storyteller is clearly part of the story, as is the addressee;
- Narratives as co-constructions—not individual subjective realities;
- Narratives as situated, contextualized in relation to multiple local-cultural-historical acts/texts;
- Inquiry may articulate multiple narratives and relations.

Narrative Interviews

We have said that our relational constructionist perspective implies that all inquiry can be viewed as narrative. Explicitly, narrative inquiry often proceeds through relatively unstructured interviews. The interviewer leaves space for the other to tell his or her story in relation to some broad question such as, "Could you tell me about your experiences of the corporate change program and the changes you have tried to introduce since you arrived?" Part of the inquirer's intention is to get out of the way, so to speak, of what other wants to say in response to the question. The interviewer might also act to make explicit things such as why he or she is asking the question(s) and who may do what with the texts (Kvale 2008). From a relational constructionist perspective, these constructive acts/texts are viewed as contexts by contributing to the particular narrative that is told in the interview. At this point in the inquiry process, we would understand the interviewee's narrative as "twice constructed" (Riessman 1993); first, by selecting and punctuating some phenomenal stream of lived experience, and second, by telling about it in the interview (Riessman 1993). We should add that we might not use the terms "interview" and "interviewer" but instead "participants" or "co-researchers."

Narrative Analysis and Deconstruction

The process of construction continues when a text is transcribed from a tape recording and decisions are made about what to do, for example, with simultaneous talk, unclear words, pauses, and punctuation. It is important to note that decisions about these features are not viewed as right or wrong but as coherent within some local context. This implies that, as an inquirer, you should make the rationale for your choices clear and be aware that these decisions could have been different, thereby constructing potentially different relational realities. The transcript is analyzed, perhaps it is more appropriate to say re-constructed, in relation to contexts such as those of the inquirer's own local cultures (gender, professional, ethnic, etc.), human science discourse, narratives of purpose, and so on. And as Riessman (1993) shows so clearly, the resulting narrative is re-constructed every time someone reads it.

A postmodern and/or relational constructionist discourse implies a particular approach to narrative analysis. In general, it aims to preserve as many text-context relations as possible, to articulate muted, suppressed, and excluded voices, and in this way to re-situate dominant voices/stories, enable a play of differences, and open up new possible realities and relationships. Some speak of this as "de-construction" (Culler 1982). It involves breaking up the seeming unities in a text (the organization, the way we do things around here, etc.), questioning taken-for-granted dualities (management-employee, old timers-newcomers), pluralizing, de-entifying, de-naturalizing, re-contextualizing, and opening up new possible local practices of power (Boje 1995; Chia 1996). Boje (2001) offers some guidelines for story deconstruction. Seven interrelated tactics are proposed: search for dualities (the system/me), re-interpret the hierarchy, look for rebel voices and for the other side of the story, deny the plot, find the exception, and trace what is between the lines.

For example, Boje (1995) investigated the possibility that there might be stories about Walt Disney and the "Magic Kingdom" that did not fit the (official) universalizing tale of happiness. He explored the voices of employees and former employees, historians, and others who might rupture the official narrative about Disney. He was interested in these alternative narratives and how competing voices were silenced and excluded. The focus of his inquiry was on the multiple and contentious relations between stories, and on how research might become complicit in constructing one happy story over the competing voices. Boje used the Disney archives, including tape and video recordings of Disney leaders making speeches, giving interviews, impromptu conversations, PR films, and tapes of meetings.

He deconstructed these texts. For example, he looked at multiple variations of stories, not just positive and not just negative. Examining the various versions, he explored how alternative stories (1) covered up a great deal of ambiguity, (2) gave voice to some and not others (e.g., absence of screen credits for artists, removal of Roy Disney from the studio sign), and (3) essentialized people and things. He did this by looking at cacophony and discord rather than "the managed harmony of the official story" and by showing organizational culture as fragmented and conflicted. Thus, the organization was now seen as a site of multiple meanings engaged in a constant struggle for control.

Working Narratives, Multiplicity, and Power To

In our relational constructionist approach, inquiry and intervention can be quite deliberately interwoven. So, for example, we can work with texts in a variety of ways that have the explicit intention of development or change. Inquiry may facilitate what Gill (2001) calls "design conversations," in which multiple voices/narratives are explored through dialogue. The varying voices and stories are not explored for purposes of selecting the best or the 'right' one, nor are they explored in order to merge them into one narrative. Rather, the purpose of opening dialogue among varying stories is to give space to each local coherence and, for example, open up possible re-storying.

Other relevant ways of working within texts can include working with metaphors (Barrett and Cooperrider 1990; Barrett, Thomas, and Hocevar 1995; see Chapter 5), "dialoging" (Anderson-Wallace, Blantern, and Boydell 2001), generating and supporting narrative multiplicity through "appreciative inquiry" (Cooperrider and Srivastva 1987), and dynamic narrative approaches to organizational learning (Abma 2000). Ways of working can also help others (clients in therapy, organizations, and communities) to generate their own ways to go on and help them to avoid presuming a singular expertise and voice. Work of this sort assumes that (a) people's lives are heavily influenced by the stories they tell about themselves; (b) stories are empowering or dis-empowering, helpful or unhelpful; (c) people may be trapped in stories of "problems" and "helplessness," past failures, and so forth that pathologize the self; and (d) both the 'change agent's' and the client's stories should be listened to and reflected back to assist dis-solving and re-storying.

Drawing on the narrative work of Michael White and David Epston (1990), David Barry's (1997) work with organizations is a good example of working with narratives to develop 'power to' go on in ways the locals find more helpful. Following White and Epston, David focuses on identities and relationships. He explored "influence mapping," "problem externalization," "identifying unique outcomes," and practices of "witnessing."

In influence mapping, people expand their stories, giving them a more coherent, story-like nature. This helps tellers assume a more agentic role. He maps the interrelations between persons and problems over time, thereby mapping the influence of 'the problem' on persons (how his problem has influenced a person's or group's life, organization, etc., perhaps making the problem less monolithic and factual). He also engages in a mapping of persons on the problem (how a person has influenced the problem or when the person has controlled or limited the problem, thereby giving a greater sense of agency).

In externalizing the problem, a storied problem is narrated as a trap. The aim here is to employ reflective listening to dis-connect the story from the teller. A person no longer "has" a problem but is now storied as "being under the 'spell' or 'control' of the problem. In this way, conversation can open on the circumstances under which the problem "takes hold" of the person as well as circumstances under which the person "beats" the problem. The relationship between person and problem is thus highlighted as opposed to centering a story of a person for whom the problem is part of self or character.

Identifying unique outcomes entails finding previously untold story parts (e.g., when some competitor or context did not get the better of them) and expanding this alternative story line. Participants can be encouraged, as well, to imagine, envision, or create a collaborative dream. Finally, witnessing performance(s) acknowledge and encourage storytellers' efforts to enact a preferred story by, for example, proposing new conversations, writing letters of reference to clients, asking for reflections from a broader group of stakeholders, and so forth.

Storytelling brings out and works with multiple voices—with multiple constructions—rather than obscuring the multiplicity in totalizing discourses, averages, third person reports, de-contextualised accounts, and other practices that aim to speak for 'other.' Storytelling change-work analyzes or in some other way 'starts from' the assumptions, norms, metaphors, language tools, and social practices that resource and constrain possibilities. Work of this kind can open up new ways of being in relation and new possible worlds.

Discourse and Discourse Analysis

Approaches that use the term discourse are not necessarily very different from narrative approaches. The distinction between the two is most easily understood in terms of whose work has been central in crafting the particular "language game" and related "forms of life." Discourse studies examine how relational processes create structures of power and authority that we treat as already existing and outside of us.

Some forms of discourse analysis focus on dominant discourses and our own participation in their (re)creation. These forms often draw on the work of Michel Foucault (1972, 1979). For example, we could examine the ways in which our own use (perhaps as patients) of the medical profession's discourse of diagnosis serves to simultaneously maintain the authority of the medical profession and entrap us in stigmatizing and pathologizing descriptions. As we define ourselves as 'depressed,' for instance, we participate in the perpetuation of "disciplinary regimes" that control and subjugate our very being. Other approaches are less interested in what Foucault calls "institutional power" or "institutional practices." Instead, they attend to taken-for-granted ways of acting in communities. Whether influenced by Foucault or, for example, Potter and Wetherell (1987), discourse studies explore how participants themselves create and sustain the practical and moral orders within which they live. Exploration of the very patterns by which such ordered ways of living emerge can allow participants to enter into new forms of relation, thereby generating possibilities for social transformation.

In relational constructionist inquiry, we are drawn to discourse or discourse analysis because we center language-based construction processes. Foucault (1972) describes discourse as "practices that form the objects of which they speak" (49). In keeping with Foucault's idea of discourse as practice, Potter and Hepburn (2008) use the term discourse by claiming it "as a verb rather than a noun" (276). A discourse can be thought of as any taken-for-granted way of talking and acting more generally that instantiates that which we assume (or take for granted) exists.

Some Examples of Discourse Analysis

In his discussion of radical approaches in psychology, Parker (2005) summarizes four key ideas of discourse analysis: multi-voicedness, semiotic construction, resistance to power, and discourse as a chain of words and images. Looking for multi-voicedness involves searching out multiple and perhaps contradictory themes rather than expecting or looking for a singular theme. Semiotic construction directs our attention to *both* how we make meaning together and how that meaning constructs us. "The description of oneself or someone else as suffering from 'mental illness,' for example, may not only construct an image of the self as a medical object but also construct a certain kind of career through the mental health system" (Parker 2005, 90). Parker sees exploring resistance to power as "a way of illuminating how language keeps certain power relations in place or challenges them" (90). We might ask, for example, if there were moments in the discourse being analyzed where the participant was able to reject a label or categorization being offered by some authoritarian voice. And last, when viewed as a chain of words and images, the concept of discourse allows us to talk about, understand, and know this and not that.

Returning to Temi's story in Chapter 1, we might suggest that he explore the ways of talking and other kinds of action (discourses, see above) that kept Mutunga from being tested for HIV/AIDS when he first started feeling ill. In opening conversation/inquiry in Mutunga's community about when it is appropriate and inappropriate to be tested, Temi and community members might not only come to learn the practices that dominate this community, but he might also invite community members to articulate the taken-for-granted discourses that they re-create in their daily activities. Temi and others could also explore the ways in which local health centers publicize HIV/AIDS testing (or the ways in which they do not publicize such testing). How are those wishing to be tested expected to make known their desire? Can they request testing in a confidential setting or must such a request take place in public? This could be seen as an example of a Foucauldian approach to discourse and discourse analysis. It could be seen as a way of "unmask[ing] oppressive discursive practices and resist[ing] dominant constructions that obscure, silence, or marginalize lived experiences that fall outside the 'mainstream' " (Foster and Bochner 2008, 94).

As we said earlier, we are not talking about precise and fully codifiable methods. Potter and Wetherell (1987) provide helpful guidelines for discourse analysis. But, of course, these reflect their discourse of science. They stress that discourse analysis is best learned through doing. When using discourse analysis as an approach to inquiry, we might carefully read documents, letters, and e-mails. We might read transcripts or interviews, look at a video tape, observe the practices of health centers, and ask ourselves, "How else might someone make sense of this?" "In what ways does this particular reading of the interaction position (e.g., pathologize) participants?" In the context of our relational constructionist perspective, what is important is some sort of critical engagement with the taken-for-granted practices and understandings, exploring how these might be otherwise. It is in these sorts of analyses that the multiple and diverse communities of participants and inquirers can collaborate to generate alternative understandings.

Again, as with narrative and all other 'methods,' discourse analysis can be approached from some sort of post-positivist or critical view of science. Here, like narrative analysis, researchers assume that they can (probably) correctly identify discourses, for example, that oppress, pathologize, legitimize, and sanction certain ways of being in certain contexts. The science orientation of the inquirer may distinguish among conceptual language/ written texts (as discourse), discursive practices, and the 'wider' societal context and focus (Fairclough 1989; van Dijk 2008). We feel that it is important to be attentive to any impulse to employ discourse analysis as a way to fix things and to prove a point. *The relational constructionist attempts to use discourse analysis to open up alternative practices that the locals find more helpful for their own local forms of life.*

Interviewing

We have often encountered two potentially conflicting notions about interviews. One is the quick association that some make between interviews and constructionism. If I conduct an interview, I am a constructionist. But as we have said, there is no constructionist method, and there is no method that is not constructed. The second conflicting idea about interviews is the common practice of using interview texts as the basis for making positive knowledge claims ("I found that . . ."). We have certainly found ourselves making such claims! For us, what is central in our orientation toward interviews is our assumption of co-construction, our interest in multiplicity, and the possibility that inquiry may transform the participating forms of life.

One illustration of interviewing practices that reflect our relational constructionist stance is the relational (or circular as they were originally called) questioning of the Milan Associates (Selvini et al. 1980; Tomm 1985). Here, the basic idea is to ask questions that generate a relationship. These forms of questions are based on Gregory Bateson's (1972) idea that information is a difference and a difference is a relationship. Thus, if we ask, "How long have you been depressed?" the answer ("three months") is likely to be viewed as factual. Yet, if we ask, "If I asked your wife how long you have been depressed, what do you think she would say?" the answer provides information about the relationship ("She would say one month," to which the wife, with a surprised look on her face responds, "Really? You think that I would say that?"). The conversation is directed to the relationship among ideas, people, contexts, and so on and away from a fact-finding expedition. We are no longer 'digging for the truth' but are now engaged in the language game of opening up multiple descriptions. Relational questioning allows participants to become reflective observers of their own relationships (the wife in the prior example says, "I never realized you thought I had that understanding of you"). With such observation comes the possibility for transformation.

Another illustration can be found in the collaborative language approach of Harlene Anderson (1997). Anderson's interviews are guided by what she refers to as a "not knowing" stance. What she means by this is that the interviewer is "not too quick to know." Although we might assume that we understand the other (particularly if we are the professional and the other is seeking our help), Anderson warns us to approach each interview with curiosity and uncertainty. The task is to invite the participant to tell his or her story without the interviewer assuming she or he already understands.

Last, we should add that much of what we said earlier about postmodern approaches to narrative and discourse is also relevant here. This means that we see the interview or conversation as an ongoing relational process that is co-constructed. It further means that the interview text is treated as a relational (and not individual) text—as a dialogical, multi-voiced performance.

Ethnography

Ethnography is very often employed as a 'method' in relation to a positive science discourse. As a method, it entails close study, through participation, of a culture or community. Although it is most often associated with cultural anthropology, ethnography is commonly used in organizational studies, education, communication, and healthcare. The ethnographer records the history of his or her observations of community practices. Of course, the significant question is: Who is privileged to record and interpret the practices of a community or culture? Within positive science, the ethnographer brings an already formed science perspective that assists him or her to make sense of observations. In addition, the ethnographer relies on "cultural informants" to describe and explain local practices and makes sense of them in relation to his or her own narratives or discourses. Alvesson and Deetz (2000) would call the latter an "elite/a priori" approach.

Given our relational stance, it is not necessary for us to impose some preconceived theory, conceptual framework, hypothesis, or content-specified interest on other. We would rather be attentive to who stands as a cultural informant and for what purposes. In their presentation of constructionist approaches to inquiry, Holstein and Gubrium (2008) note:

> constructionist analytics recognize that reality constituting "language games" (Wittgenstein 1953) are frequently institutionalized, which sets the practical conditions for talk and interaction. The experientially real is simultaneously and reflexively constitutive of, and constituted through, ongoing social relations. Constructionist ethnographers gaze both at and beyond immediate discursive activity to examine the ways in which broader—if still socially constructed—circumstances, conditions, and interpretive resources mediate the reality-construction process. (376)

A further extension of ethnography adopted within a relational constructionist stance could be auto-ethnography. Ellis (2004) defines auto-ethnography as "research, writing, story, and method that connect the autobiographical and personal to the cultural, social and political" (xix). Gergen and Gergen (2003) see auto-ethnography as allowing us to become " 'witnesses' . . . rather than reporting on 'subjects under observation,' the auto-ethnographer serves as the subject . . . giv[ing] first-hand insight into a form of life, making it available to the broader community" (62). In the auto-ethnographies we have seen, critical self-reflection is central, opening multiple voices/multiple interpretations and generating new action potentials for the inquirer and for the reader.

In our view, ethnography and auto-ethnography could be developed in ways that more fully realize the potential of a relational constructionist perspective. Some approaches move in this direction by claiming a "critical" orientation (Carspecken 1996; Thomas 1993). For Thomas, this means "conventional ethnography with a political purpose" (4). He continues, "conventional ethnographers study culture for the purpose of describing it; critical ethnographers do so to change it" by opening up alternative possibilities (40). Issues of dialogical relations, power and dominance, ethics and multiple (community-based) voices stand central in this line of work (Conquergood 1997; Madison 2005). There are also examples of auto-ethnography that center multiple relational voices and offer new ways of being in relation. For example, Fox (1996) integrates multiple voices in her analysis of child sexual abuse. She includes her own voice as both researcher and former victim of sexual abuse, the voice of the sex offender, and the voice of the victim in an attempt to expose the multiple orientations to child sexual abuse. Last, and most consistent with our relational constructionist perspective, some take the view that any critical inquiry should also include an auto-ethnographic element (Hosking 2008; Howeling 2011).

Reflections

When preparing for any form of inquiry, we are confronted with a host of decisions. From a traditional research orientation, our choices distinguish our work as good science or bad science. Yet, when research/inquiry is approached as a process of relational construction, our choices are "fateful" but not necessarily right or wrong, good or bad. Because we are speaking out of and into diverse language communities, the meaning of our inquiry and our choices will vary.

- *How might this orientation liberate you to engage with others involved in ways that are more sensitive and responsive to the multiple local rationalities?*
- *Try re-storying your current or some previous investigation in terms of (a postmodern orientation to) narrative, discourse, and ethnography. What different possibilities does each open up?*

LOOKING BACK

What we have tried to offer in this chapter is an understanding that, when we lean toward inquiry as constructionists, there are ways of positioning ourselves in relation to our work. This orientation and positioning becomes more important than any particular method. We consider methods as forms of practice. Each form of practice opens some possibilities and closes others, just as does the choice of method in positive science. Yet, unlike positive science, where the selection of a method is evaluated as being good or bad—given the research question, scientific interest, and so forth—within a constructionist sensibility, the selection of a form of practice is considered a potentially relationally responsive act. It now becomes possible to attempt to practice inquiry with (rather than on) participants who act in relation to multiple different but equal local realities.

We think it is important to remember that the features that pull us toward narrative, discourse, interviewing, and ethnography (or some other form[s]) are the multi-voiced, thick-textured, relationally engaged practices they allow. To the constructionist, a method is a resource for engagement. Being relationally engaged means that, for us, there is no neutral stance—there is no "god's eye view" from nowhere (Putnam 1990). Each move in the relational dance of inquiry emerges out of and contributes to co-constructed practical and moral orders and relations—whether or not the relations are equal.

Table 4.1 Shifts in Thinking About Inquiry

Received view of science	Relational constructionism
Data	On-going Process
Results	Process
Control	Minimal structures & unfolding
Method	Forms of practice/performance *in context*
Reliability	Generativity
Validity	Usefulness to the (multiple) local communities
Protocol	Emergence & reflexivity
Science & scientist centered	Ongoing processes centered

Some of the significant shifts we make in understanding the process of inquiry as relational constructionists are summarized in Table 4.1.

In the next chapter, we explore the ways in which our inquiry processes transform the worlds we inhabit as well as the worlds of those who participate in our inquiry. We offer some useful illustrations of transformative work as elaborated by participative action research, appreciative inquiry, and transformative dialogue processes.

5 Transforming Inquiries
Enlarging Possible Worlds

"It is a long tail, certainly."

INTRODUCTION

We ended Chapter 4 with a table summarizing the process of inquiry as we understand it given our relational constructionist 'meta-theory.' To recap, in Chapter 4 we made the point that, in principle, we can use anything that positive science would call a 'method.' What relational constructionism offers us is an understanding that the way we think about methods and the way we use, talk, and write about them always emerge from a particular meta-theory. And, as we have shown, all meta-theories make assumptions about what exists (ontology), what we can know about what exists (epistemology), and how we can produce that knowledge (methodology). What becomes central for the constructionist is how we use any particular method. Our assumptions guide the questions we ask, how we try to answer them, what we count as 'data,' what we count as 'fact,' the language tools we use, what we recognize as rigor, and so on.

Our views on process and on 'the question of method' apply equally to the subject of this chapter: transforming inquiries. We are playing with words here. One of the meanings we are playing with is that, given our relational constructionist stance, inquiry can be transformed into something more like 'intervention' or 'change work.' Of course, the other meaning is that inquiry can, indeed, be transformed. Put otherwise, inquiry ('method') can be transformed from our post-positivist ways of understanding it and/or inquiry, itself, can be transformative because we view inquiry as an ongoing process in which relational realities are (re)constructed. This point is often missed by those whose narratives of inquiry are (unbeknown to them) constrained by a view of science that is not relational constructionist. Depending on the community we are speaking to or writing for, we might use the language of inquiry or we might use terms such as development, evaluation (see Chapter 6), or change work.

Our focus in this chapter is on the potentially transformative aspects of inquiry. In this context, we use the term 'transformative' to refer to change that unfolds 'from within,' in patterns of relating over time (Watzlawick, Weakland, and Fisch 1974), where the 'unfolding' goes on in different but equal (not subject-object) relations that are better described as (re) constructing 'power to' rather than 'power over' (Hosking 2000, 2004). Power is a term that might be used to speak of the unfolding relations between different local-communal rationalities. In subject-object ways of relating, one rationality dominates others (here we speak of "power over"), and the 'what' and 'how' of relating is imposed 'from the outside,' so to speak. When relating goes on in softer self-other differentiation, the different participating 'forms of life' have 'power to' unfold from within their own local rationality (in different but equal relations).

Returning to our discussion of inquiry possibilities in Chapter 1, we can see that both Temi (working with AIDS) and Femke (consulting on age-related practices in an organization) had the possibility to 'lean' more toward inquiry (in the more common sense of 'research as [mediated] discovery') or, indeed, to 'lean' more toward transformation. They could have done the latter by innovating new 'methods' or by crafty use of existing methods—all the while guided by the relational constructionist discourse. Returning to our introduction, we are suggesting that a transformed approach to inquiry can 'lean' more toward transformative ways of 'going on' in relation—the subject of this chapter. This said, the distinction between the inquiry orientations we outlined in the previous chapter (i.e., narrative, discourse and discourse analysis, interviewing, and ethnography) and the approaches we will describe in this chapter can best be articulated as the difference between "approaches we might use in our inquiries" (Chapter 4) and "ways of engaging with communities that employ some of these approaches in a particular manner with the explicit understanding that self and other will be transformed" (the present Chapter).

We will discuss potentially transformative orientations to inquiry first by outlining some existing approaches, including Action Science (Reason and Torbert 2001), Participative Action Research (Fals-Borda and Rahman 1991), and Appreciative Inquiry (Cooperrider and Srivastva 1987). We then go on to focus on dialogical practices and their role in transformative change work. We conclude this chapter with an articulation of some "orienting themes" (as opposed to "methods") that we have found helpful in enlarging possible worlds.

EXISTING APPROACHES TO TRANSFORMATIVE CHANGE

Action Science

Peter Reason and Bill Torbert (2001), two key players in approaches that center participation, action, and transformation, re-vision human science practices and interests in the following way:

> since all human persons are participating actors in their world, the purpose of inquiry is . . . to forge a more direct link between intellectual knowledge and moment to moment personal and social action, so that

inquiry contributes directly to the flourishing of human persons, their communities, and the ecosystems of which they are a part. (4–5)

This means that their interest lies in how to inquire in the midst of action and how to create communities of inquiry within what we have been calling local forms of life.

In this context, Reason and Torbert highlight four key aspects or "dimensions" of inquiry. The first is a "primary purpose" oriented toward "practical knowing" embodied in moment-to-moment actions. The second is that human knowing is essentially participative—grounded in ongoing relations with other persons and "in the wider ecology of living and non-living things" (6). In this sense, and like relational constructionism, they see all action as inter-action and view all research as participatory, relational, political, and ecological. The third dimension is that inquiry and all knowing are "based in the sensing, feeling, thinking, attending experiential presence of persons in their world" (6). The experiential encounter is "tacit, pre-verbal, inchoate" and "prior to both description and the object described" (9). Fourth, all moment-to-moment actions embrace some sort of "normative theory of what act is timely now" (6). Broadly speaking, this refers to an orientation toward some desired future for one's community and relations with others.

We find many resonances here with our practical interests and ways of working. Perhaps especially helpful is what Reason and Torbert offer as strategies for transformative inquiry. In what they called first person research/practice, the inquirer 'goes upstream' to reflect on and explore his or her own patterns and purposes—his or her own histories and the ways he or she reproduces them. So, for example, our reflective practitioner might find it helpful to employ practices such as auto-ethnography, therapeutic conversation, storying and re-storying, martial arts, and meditation.

Another strategy could be what they called second person research/practice, which involves joining with others in a face-to-face group to build on first person inquiries. One example, "co-operative inquiry" (Heron 1996) involves groups of inquirers who act as co-researchers co-constructing all aspects of the inquiry and engaging in cycles of reflection on their own experiences and learning. Approaches that center (appreciative) dialogues or use the language of "participatory action research" (Fals-Borda and Rahman 1991) could be said to include such "second person" practices.

Finally, the strategy of third person research/practice aims to create a wider community of inquiry, one in which participants collaborate to create their own knowing-in-action and to influence other groups such as those involved in, for example, planning and creating government policy (see also Torbert 2000). Work of this sort includes democratic dialogues and dialogue conferences (Toulmin and Gustavsen 1996), whole systems approaches (Bunker and Alban 1997; New Economics Foundation 1998), collaborative inquiry (Anderson and Gehart 2007), future search (Weisbord and Janoff 1995), participatory development (Chambers 1994), appreciative inquiry (Cooperrider and Srivastva 1987), and many others. We will say a little about two examples—participatory action research and appreciative inquiry. We will also discuss dialogical practices because they play an important role in all such work.

Participative Action Research

What was simply called action research traditionally focused on the scientific researcher and, through him or her, the norms, values, and interests of (some variant of) positive science. What makes this form of action research research is the practice of feeding back the research 'findings' to the community from which they have been produced so that this feedback can guide subsequent actions or interventions, such as planned organizational development (Cummings and Worley 2001). This tradition has been re-constructed and revised in a variety of ways, for example, to include organizational applications of participatory action research (Greenwood, Whyte, and Harkavy 1993), action science (Argyris, Putnam, and Smith 1985), and appreciative inquiry (Cooperrider and Srivastva 1987).

Participative action research (PAR) is given quite different meanings by different groups of practitioners. We focus here on what some have called the "southern tradition" (Reason and Torbert 2001). It takes a radical 'liberationist' stance that gives central importance to what Foucault (1980) called the knowledge/power nexus. This sort of PAR is oriented around the "enlightenment and awakening of common peoples" (Fals-Borda and Rahman 1991, vi) whose local-cultural practices, experiences, and knowledges are often ignored, muted, or devalued by outside interest groups, including science.

Key concepts and practices of this version of PAR include ways of working that provide all participants with what Fals-Borda and Rahman call direct "experience" of organizing rather than having their participation limited to data provision. The term "experience" is being given a very particular meaning, one perhaps better expressed by the Spanish term *vivencia*. This concept embraces the notion of getting in touch with otherness—not just with the 'mind' but "with the heart" (Fals-Borda and Rahman 1991, 11). Fals-Borda and Rahman link this notion with "authentic commitment." The key to PAR (in this sense) is constructing practical commitment to a process that transforms relations from subject-object to "subject-subject" (5)—a process of "building 're-enchantment bridges' " (32) between science/academic knowledge and local knowledge(s) or "folk science." Authentic participation is viewed as a dialogical practice—a "horizontal" practice—that "affirm(s) the importance of the Other" (33). It involves respecting differences and allowing different voices to be heard; feeling the 'extopian,' as Mikhail Bakhtin (1986) would say. When we discover ourselves in others, we affirm our own identity and culture and attune ourselves to a vivified cosmos (33).

In sum, this philosophy and practice of PAR clearly appreciates multiple local rationalities and supports their coming together and working in different but equal relations. Inquiry and intervention, knowledge and power, knowledge and action, and heart and mind are seen as intimately interwoven.

Emergent processes of collaboration and dialogue are emphasized, as are the role and importance of openness to other—seen as part of, rather than apart from, self. PAR, at least in the view of Reason and Torbert, clearly involves transforming self-other relations together with whole-hearted participation grounded in a 'heart connection.' In our view, the philosophy of PAR, and transformational action science more generally, hold great potential for relationally engaged forms of praxis, and the interested reader is encouraged to read case examples to get a better feel of how PAR might 'go on' in practice.

Reflection

Consider: You are interested in decision-making processes within a local community. You have decided that PAR would be a generative way to engage this community in self-exploration and eventual transformation. Imagine the different ways in which your inquiry would construct alternative possibilities if you used:

- *Narrative interviews*
- *Narrative analysis and deconstruction*
- *Discourse analysis*
- *Interviewing*
- *Ethnography*

Of course, none of these approaches is objectively better than another. Yet consider how the local-cultural processes might make one (or more) approach more coherent or more helpful than another(s).

Appreciative Inquiry

As we said earlier, both appreciative inquiry (AI) and PAR have been described as a modification of traditional action research (Cummings and Worley 2001; Reason 1994). In AI, just as in PAR, the scientist or outside expert aims to bring his or her local-cultural practices to work with other local cultures in ways that give space to multiple local-cultural interests and ways of knowing. However unlike PAR and other development approaches, AI—from the start—was explicitly grounded in a relational constructionist meta-theory. To elaborate a little, in one of the earliest articulations of AI, David Cooperrider reflected on the kinds of realities and relations people create when they view reality as 'out there,' self-existing, and knowable, for example, through (action) research. As we have seen, this kind of (modernist) discourse separates self (in here) from other (out there)—other people, the government, the environment, and so on. It further positions self as a knower of these self-existing entities and as one who can e-value-ate realities and relations as good or bad, right or wrong. Constructions of this sort invite attention to finding out about (i.e., diagnosing, assessing) and intervening to 'fix' things that are bad or wrong. As we showed in Chapter

2, the modernist discourse separates inquiry and intervention, positions experts as those who must diagnose and fix problems, and perpetuates what we have been calling S-O (subject-object, self-other) relations.

Reasoning from a relational constructionist perspective, Cooperrider and his colleagues proposed a way of working that *does not* orient around the assumption of a world of problems, deficiencies, and deficits—an assumption that characterizes many traditional approaches to change, for example, in discourses of organization development. Instead, AI is oriented around (local) values and valued futures, around what gives life and energy to the participants. In the words of Cooperrider and Srivastva (1987), the term AI "refers to both a search for knowledge and a theory of intentional collective action which are designed to help evolve the normative vision and will of a group, organization, or society as a whole" (159). We should stress that even though futures are emphasized, working with AI within a relational constructionist discourse suggests that AI is seen as a 'here and now' process of constructing realties and relations (the path *is* the product).

Early writings on AI set out some guidelines or steps that we could think of as some sort of "minimal structuring" (see Chapter 4) of the inquiry process. Asking questions is given a central role. But asking questions is not the exclusive right of the researcher, for the purpose of finding out about what already *is* (as in the modernist science discourse of research). Instead, many people are afforded the opportunity to ask and answer questions and, in the process, to generate "a positive core" that constitutes an ongoing resource for the inquiry.

AI work features a '4-D' cycle (or some variation of the same) that could be a way of thinking about a single conversation, a yearlong community development initiative, or a large-scale organizational inquiry involving the participation of multiple stakeholders. The 4-D cycle consists of a flow among discovery of what we find life-giving, of what we appreciate (discussion of which generates the "positive core"); dreaming about what we might become—in a clear, pragmatic way—given these positive resources; designing our ideal organization—one that could realize these dreams; and destiny in the sense of working with issues such as how to empower, learn, and improvise to enable and sustain these processes.

This cycle has as its core the choice of an affirmative topic. As we noted earlier in our discussion of generic themes, the choice of the question is absolutely key because it has a formative role in what is made 'real and good'—in the realities that are co-constructed (in both the process and in terms of what is given attention and resources). In other words, the affirmative topic is key to the transformative potential of the process. In one example, while working with a healthcare system spread geographically over a large city, tensions about the distribution of limited resources arose. Each satellite office had different needs because of the different populations of each geographic area. Rather than initiate a consultation where the problem was analyzed, the consultant engaged the group in a storytelling process that invited each satellite office to talk about itself at its best. By beginning with an affirmative topic, the predictable battle over which office was the more needy or more deserving of additional resources transformed into a conversation infused with curiosity, inspiration, and connection. Participants created bonds of connection as opposed to distancing relations focused solely on the distribution of limited resources (McNamee 1998).

Perhaps it is worth repeating that we are not talking about a 'method' here. AI 'puts to work' a particular human science discourse (relational constructionism) in a practical, potentially transformative approach to inquiry (Hosking and McNamee 2007). Any particular instance might use various 'methods,' including interviews and perhaps questionnaires and existing databases, and might include the use of non-conceptual forms such art or music making (recall Shayamal's story in Chapter 4). Similarly, it is possible to find cases reported as "AI" that distinguish six steps (rather than four), use terms other than "discovery, dream, design, and destiny," or join an appreciative orientation with other approaches such as "participatory rural appraisal" (Chambers 1994).

To us, it is important to highlight the key themes of (1) de-centering the community of science relative to other local communities, (2) centering dialogue (or rather multiple dialogues), and (3) centering (usually implicitly) 'power to' rather than 'power over' (Gergen 1995; Hosking 1995)—as the processes construct possibilities for participants to go on in different but equal relation. Perhaps this is a good time to say something more about dialogical practices and their role in transforming inquiries.

Reflection

Thinking about your own inquiry topic, how might you:

- *De-center the community of science relative to other local communities?*
- *Center multiple dialogues?*
- *Center 'power to' rather than 'power over'?*
- *Start from an appreciative stance (i.e., what is working, what is affirming, what gives life)?*

DIALOGICAL PRACTICES AND THEIR ROLE IN CHANGE WORK

References to dialogue have become increasingly popular in connection with relationally engaged, transformative change work. Work of this sort includes appreciative inquiry (Cooperrider and Srivastva 1987) and 'collaborative consulting' (Anderson 1997), which are grounded in a relational or dialogical view of person and processes, and PAR, most often grounded in a humanist and/or participative worldview (Reason and Bradbury 2001).

All these approaches share in the attempt to open up 'power to' rather than close down through 'power over.' They do so through (1) working through multiple conversations, often referred to as "dialogues," rather than single-voiced leadership edicts and the avoidance of talk and discussion; (2) working with many different self-other relations, rather than a single hierarchy of knowledge and expertise; (3) working with what is already (potentially) available and with 'stuff' that the participants believe to be relevant, rather than imposing mono-logical constructions of leaders or, for example, outside experts; and (4) inviting and supporting many lines of action rather than requiring or imposing consensus. These sorts of dialogical processes can facilitate multiple community-based voices and can help multiple communities (as 'forms of life') participate such that other realities can be 'allowed to lie' rather than being questioned, grasped, judged, and re-constructed by a particular, knowing, and structuring agent.

Other relevant social science approaches explicitly center and emphasize dialogue, and they give it a very special meaning. Here, we are thinking of the Public Conversations Project (PCP) (Chasin et al. 1996), work using the language of 'transformative dialogues' (Gergen, McNamee, and Barrett 2001), 'dialogue conferences' (Toulmin and Gustavsen 1996), and the MIT dialogue project (Isaacs 1993, 2001; Senge 1990). These approaches draw on rather different (although related) theoretical traditions that have emerged in different communities. So, for example, Toulmin and Gustavsen, Isaacs, Senge, and others draw from the work of the theoretical physicist David Bohm (Bohm and Nichol 2004), whereas PCP and "transformative dialogue" draw more from communication theory and family therapy (Watzlawick, Bavelas, and Jackson 1967).

All of these approaches narrow their use of the term dialogue to refer to a very special kind of conversation and not to 'just' any kind of talk. As a special kind of conversation, dialogue is a slow, open, and curious way of relating characterized by (1) a very special kind of listening, questioning, and being present; (2) a willingness to suspend assumptions and certainties; and (3) reflexive attention to the ongoing process. So, rather than constructing separate, fixed, or closed realities, for example, of self (other) and one's own (others) position on some issue, dialogical practices open up to relationality and to possibilities, and open up space for self and other to co-emerge in different but equal relations (what Bohm calls flow). We will say a little about Bohm's work and the MIT dialogue project, as well as PCP.

Bohm and Dialogue

David Bohm's work on dialogue has been drawn on extensively in areas of organization development, most notably in the work of Peter Senge, Bill Isaacs, and others for whom dialogue became a key component in the creation of the learning organization (Isaacs 1993, 2001; Senge 1990), together with later work on "presence" and "theory U" (Senge et al. 2005). Bohm was an eminent theoretical physicist whose work led him to a holistic and ongoing or processual view of reality. He talked about the coherence and/or incoherence of ongoing processes/realities. For him, processes are viewed as incoherent when people position themselves apart from the whole, try to understand wholeness through abstract thought, and hold on to fixed assumptions and judgments. In his view,

> incoherence on a large scale (involves) patterns of thinking and acting that separate people from one another and from the larger reality in which they are attempting to live. (cited in Bohm 2004, x)

This line of talk resonates with what we earlier described as entitative thinking and subject-object relations, whether in daily life, community, therapeutic and organizational change work, or science. In this connection, Bohm saw science and western rationalism as contributing to incoherence by assuming and orienting towards finding some unique truth.

Dialogue comes into the present discussion as a process that can reveal inconsistencies in people's stances and that can support exploration of what hinders communication (ways of relating) between, for example, different parts of some organization or between different nations. Through the practice of dialogue, coherent ways of thinking and acting can emerge through processes that allow multiplicity (e.g., multiple points of view) and movement or "flow." According to Bohm, these sorts of processes allow participants to "take part in truth." His "thought style" or meta-theory (Chapter 2) is participative; it is participating consciousness that allows people to understand the whole. This same view is found reflected in Reason and Torbert's talk of practical, participative knowing or participative consciousness (Reason 1994; Reason and Torbert 2001).

Bohm's thought style could also be called dialogical (Bohm and Nichol 2004); dialogue allows participants to experience (what we earlier called) relational realities as continually unfolding and to see themselves as contributors. This line of talk resonates with what we earlier called "soft self-other differentiation," with our suggestion that transformative change requires a dialogical view of personhood and with our call for a shift from entitative to relationally engaged ways of working.

In *Dialogue—A Proposal*, Bohm and his co-authors argue that dialogue:

> . . . is a way of exploring the roots of the many crises that face humanity today. It enables inquiry into, and understanding of, the sorts of processes that fragment and interfere with real communication between individuals, nations and even different parts of the same organization. (Bohm, Factor, and Garrett 1991)

Dialogue provides a container for slowing down speedy 'internal' and 'external' conversations, grooved patterns, unquestioned assumptions, and conventional tendencies to fragment or to break things up that are not really separate. It provides space for the display of these fragmentations (we might say entifications), for friction between different values and assumptions, for listening, for reflexive practices, and for attention to the 'how' of relational processes. Attention in the form of non-judgmental curiosity becomes a vitally important practice. Over a period of time, these sorts of dialogical practices enable and support (1) presence or now-ness (rather than holding on to past convictions and prejudices), (2) emergent possibilities and insights (flow rather than solidification), (3) collective learning (rather than individual knowledge gain), and (4) a sense of participating in wholeness (rather than separate existences).

For Bohm, the practice of dialogue is an exploratory and emergent or unfolding process without any apparent goal other than collective exploration. It differs from other conversational forms such as discussion and right/wrong debate; it is not intended as group therapy, and it is definitely not the same as dinner party entertainment.

Bohm, Factor, and Garret (1991) suggest that dialogue works best with twenty to forty people seated in a circle. The purpose of the activity is introduced along the lines outlined earlier. The group will usually meet together on a series of occasions, beginning with any topic of interest to participants. In the early stages, some facilitation is usually needed to help the group become aware of itself and its relational dynamics. However, dialogue is intended to be a conversation of equals. Although there are no fixed rules or methods, a key practice is "suspension" of preconceived assumptions or beliefs by giving attention to the ongoing relational processes and one's own part in them. This is achieved by paying attention, listening to one's self and others, and exposing one's own thoughts and feelings to reflection. In these ways, participants are able to see how they participate in constructing the realities that they believe to be facts, are able to see that their constructions could be otherwise, and are able to experience relationality. Dialogues of this sort can allow a new kind of "coherent, collective intelligence" to emerge (Bohm, Factor, and Garrett 1991). We might say that dialogue, in this sense, can be seen as a potentially transformative inquiry practice.

Reflection

As you think about your own inquiry processes, in what ways does your approach:

- *Enable and work with what is happening 'in the moment?'*
- *Invite emergent possibilities—constructions 'not yet realized?'*
- *Assume community-based constructions as opposed to individual knowledge?*
- *Create a sense of community as opposed to individual agency?*

The Public Conversation Project

In 1989, Laura and Richard Chasin, Sallyann Roth, and their colleagues at the Public Conversations Project (PCP) in Watertown, Massachusetts, began to apply skills developed in the context of family therapy to 'stuck' public controversies (Chasin and Herzig 1992). Their practice has evolved over the years and with impressive results. Here we focus on their attempt to bring together committed activists on opposing sides of the abortion conflict, although their work has expanded well beyond this public controversy in the past three decades to include public dialogues on same sex marriage, gun control, political divides, differences in the Middle East, and more. Abortion, like many other controversial public issues, is a case in which public debate has led nowhere largely because the opponents construct reality and morality in entirely different ways. The stakes are high, there is enormous animosity, and the consequences are lethal. What follows is a brief outline of that project.

Activists who were willing to discuss abortion with their opponents were brought together in small groups. The Project guaranteed that they would not have to participate in any activity that they found uncomfortable. The meeting began with a dinner in which the participants were asked to share various aspects of their lives other than their stand on abortion. In fact, at the pre-dialogue dinner, participants did not know who was pro-choice and who was pro-life. In other words, participants engaged in typical social conversation while they dined, reserving the topic of abortion for the post-dinner dialogue. After dinner, the facilitators invited the participants into "a different kind of conversation." They were asked to speak from their own stance, articulating their own experiences and ideas rather than speaking as representatives of a position. Additionally, they were asked to share their thoughts and feelings and to ask questions about which they were genuinely curious. As the session began, the participants were asked to respond, each in turn and without interruption, to three major questions:

* How did you get involved with this issue? What's your personal relationship or personal history with it?
* We'd like to hear a little more about your particular beliefs and perspectives about the issues surrounding abortion. What is at the heart of the matter for you?
* Many people we've talked to articulate that, within their approach to this issue, they find some gray areas, some dilemmas about their own beliefs, or even some conflicts. Do you experience any pockets of uncertainty or lesser certainty, any concerns, value conflicts, or mixed feelings that you may have and wish to share?

Answers to the first two questions typically yielded a variety of personal experiences, often stories of the participants' lives or the experiences of loved ones. Participants also revealed many doubts and found themselves surprised to learn that people on the other side of the issue have any uncertainties at all.

After addressing the three questions, participants were given an opportunity to ask questions of each other. They were not invited to ask questions that "are challenges in disguise," but to ask questions "about which you are genuinely curious . . . we'd like to learn about your own personal experiences and individual beliefs." After discussing a wide range of issues important to the participants, there was a final discussion of what the participants felt they had done to "make the conversation go as it had." Follow-up phone calls a few weeks after each session revealed significant, positive effects. Participants felt they left with a more complex understanding of the struggle and a significantly re-humanized view of "the other." No, they did not change their fundamental views, but they no longer saw the issues in such black and white terms, nor did they view those who disagreed with their own position as demons. As such, they were now poised to engage in conversation about abortion in a dialogic manner.

The PCP has a number of interesting features to which we would like to give special attention. They concern the ways in which the process is structured to open up the possibility of careful and respectful listening (remember, earlier we said that this was difficult and needed practice). One important lesson we learn from the PCP is that the preparation of self and others to participate in dialogue (and not debate) is critical. Our 'accepted' ways of relating are so routine that doing anything other than defending our own position on, for example, a controversial issue is very unlikely. In PCP, participants are prepared for dialogue by being asked to think about (1) their own personal relationship to a controversial issue, (2) who inspired or compelled them to adopt these beliefs and values, and (3) how they take shape in the flux and flow of their life history. Participants might also be asked to consider what voices they need to leave at home on the day of the dialogue in order for it to be productive and fruitful for all. In sum, without careful preparation, participants will often innocently rely on their best persuasive and argumentative strategies.

In addition to preparing participants for dialogue, it is important to create a safe context. For example, why should a pro-choice (for abortion) person feel comfortable coming into a conversational process with a pro-life (against abortion) advocate? If participants feel that care has been taken to create a physical and conversational space where differences can co-exist, they are more likely to risk entering into a conversation that is not like the ordinary defensive and persuasive debate to which they are accustomed. As you can see, there is a focused discipline in preparing participants to enter into dialogue. The expectation that one can bring people together and dialogue will emerge is risky. We like to think of dialogue as requiring an entirely different sort of space, one that enables the suspension of dogma without requiring any relinquishing of passion and commitment.

Reflection

- *If you were to invite people into a 'public conversation' as opposed to a 'debate,' how would you do that?*

In conclusion, dialogical practices that are grounded in a relational view of processes (and so, a dialogical view of person) offer an alternative to disengaged ways of being in relation. Dialogue can provide a way out of stuckness, a way out of some seemingly solid, stable, and singular 'I' who builds individual knowledge about, and seeks control over, other. Dialoging can help to bring forth and support appreciation (rather than judgment and critique), discussion of what can be done (rather than what cannot), and a sense of relational responsibility (rather than blaming individuals). Dialogue makes space for ongoing emergence, for improvisation. In practicing the 'discipline of collective inquiry,' participants learn how to learn—they learn to open up to possibilities, that is, to other constructions of what is real and good.

CONCLUSION: SOME ORIENTING THEMES

So what can we now say about work that 'leans toward' inquiry as potentially transformative—about work that is oriented toward enlarging possible worlds? Certain practice themes seem to keep re-emerging, themes that provide us with generative resources for working out how to go on in any (new) particular case. We think they could also help you when, for example, you find yourself facing the question, "How do I go on from here?" "How could I craft a process that invites and appreciates equal participation in a potentially transformative inquiry?" These "orienting themes"—clearly they are not methods—include:

- opening space for now-ness
- both knowing and influencing
- unfolding multiple local realities in different but equal relation
- respecting emergent processes and possibilities
- centering appreciation
- embracing both inquiry and intervention
- seeing both questioning and listening as potentially (trans)formative
- constructing in both conceptual and non-conceptual performances
- constructing eco-logical ways of being

These are all highly interconnected, but, for the sake of simplicity, we will adopt these analytical distinctions and say a little about each in turn.

Opening Space for Now-ness

Moving away from subject-object ways of relating requires creating ways to open up to multiple local communities and their differing norms, values, interests, ways of relating, or, in other words, their local rationalities. Centering ongoing relational processes and their transformative potential means letting go of 'first/then' constructions such as 'first inquire/know and then intervene' or 'first design/know and then implement.' Instead, our relational constructionist view of process locates the past and the future in the present (see Chapter 3). *The present, in this very special sense, is all there is.* Instead of instrumental relations between self and other, there is now-ness and its potential for transforming relational realities of self, other, and relations. There is nothing more important than the interactive moment because this moment creates the future into which we enter.

Both Knowing and Influencing

Transformative development work recognizes the potential influence of all inter-acts or co-ordinations. Part of what this involves is letting go of the assumption that an individual scientist or change agent should perform individual acts to achieve "power over" some independently existing other (Gergen 1995; Hosking 1995). Another part involves letting go of practices that separate and polarize acts of inquiry (to know) and acts of influence (to change other). In the context of relational constructionism, all ways of relating can be thought of as part of the "knowledge/power nexus" (Foucault 1980). Transformative inquiries see knowledge and power (now relationally theorized) as dancing together, so to speak. Knowledge and power are both located in ongoing relational processes, and much more emphasis is given to power than inquiries based in, for example, post-positivist science. In so doing, they give more emphasis and more value to ways of relating that construct "power to" (Gergen 2009a), which brings us to our next generic theme.

Multiple Local Realities in Different but Equal Relation

Moving away from subject-object ways of relating means opening up space for multiple local-communal forms of life and their conventional ways of relating, constructing knowledge and interests (Gergen 1994; Fals-Borda and Rahman 1991). In general terms, this suggests relating in ways that are relatively open and that give space to multiplicity. This means giving space to difference, to constructing "power to" go on in new ways, and to becoming some-one or some-thing different. This may mean trying to include all community-based rationalities that are implicated or involved in some practice or issue, for example, through "large-group interventions" (Bunker and Alban 1997) or PAR (Reason and Bradbury 2001). Giving space to difference is further developed in our next theme.

Emerging Processes and Possibilities

The view that relational processes open up and close down possibilities has major implications for all transformative change work. For example, it involves a shift of emphasis from design and planning (of some yet-to-be-implemented inquiry or intervention) to ongoing emergence, development, and preparation. Often this means working with what our colleague, Frank Barrett (2006), calls "minimal structures." These provide some sort of mid-way between 'anything goes' (too loose) and some already well worked out means and ends (too tight). A related aspect is found in ways of working that invite participants to imagine what could be and to initiate projects to actualize valued possibilities. One such approach is illustrated by Imagine Chicago, an initiative that invites participants to imagine their city and how they would like it to be (www.imaginechicago.org). Approaches that explicitly center improvisation can also be thought of in this way because, within this frame, all actions are understood as offers or invitations that are extended and that may be taken up in a process of making new realities and relations (Barrett 2006).

Centering Appreciation

Opening up to possibilities can be greatly facilitated by appreciative ways of coordinating with what is presented. In this context, appreciation means not imposing good/bad or right/wrong evaluations; evaluations are always local to a particular community. In this sense, the practice of appreciation could be related to what Corradi Fiumara (1990), drawing on Heideggar, called "letting lie" compared with grasping ("Now I've got it!"). Appreciative inquiry (Cooperrider and Srivastva 1987) gives particular importance to ways of working that, for example, support a tone of curiosity and openness to possibility, rather than judgment and fixing what was, is, or should be. Thus, appreciative questions might focus on 'what kind of community would we like to become?' rather than 'what's wrong with our community?' This orientation reflects our relational constructionist leaning away from questions and answers that fix what IT IS or re-construct failure, inadequacy, and insufficiencies by talking about and orienting around (constructions of) problems. Again we see that the ways we relate with one another, the questions we ask, and the words we use create the worlds in which we live.

Both Inquiring and Intervening

As we have said, because relational processes construct realities, there is no requirement to entify activities as either inquiry or intervention (although of course one could); instead, a 'both-and' approach is enabled. So, for example, traditional action research can be developed in more multi-voiced, participatory ways (Reason and Torbert 2001). These, along with "minimal structures" such as co-inquiry, collaborative inquiry, and appreciative inquiry, are potentially transformative (see Reason and Bradbury 2001). Similarly, "large-group interventions" such as " future search" can be re-storied as potentially valuable for what is achieved in the (ongoing) here and now (Weisbord and Janov 2000). The questions we ask invite new understandings, new possibilities for self-reflection, and new possibilities for action.

Both Questioning and Listening Are Potentially (Trans)Formative

A changed role and significance is given to asking questions, to how they are asked, why, and by whom. Rather than see questioning as 'finding out' about some pre-existing reality, questioning now is seen as formative. In addition, 'good' questions might be defined as those that help to enlarge possible worlds and possible ways of being in relationship (see Harding 1998). We suppose that it is for reasons such as these that appreciative inquiry gives careful attention to the appreciative question around which the process is based (e.g., "tell me about a high point in your organization; a time when the organization was at its best").

Listening also has a role and significance that differs from that in positive science. Listening is not about listening *for* information; instead, it is listening *with*. It is listening that stays open, that gives space to the possibility of becoming other (transformation). Probably for these reasons, listening is given a central place in many approaches that explicitly focus on dialogue (Bunker and Alban 1997; Chasin et al. 1996; Gergen, McNamee, and Barrett 2001; Isaacs 1993). We should add that listening, in this very special sense, needs a lot of practice. Participants are invited to learn how to let go of their own stories as a reference point (Hosking 2007b).

Constructing in Both Conceptual and Non-Conceptual Performances

Transformative inquiries can, for example, focus on and work with how people talk to, with, and about self and other. Such inquiries can also focus on how people or communities (including organizational theorists) employ dominant metaphors (Lakoff and Johnson 1980; Morgan 1986; Palmer and Dunford 1996), narratives or stories (Boje 1995; Czarniawska-Joerges 1997), or the language of problems or appreciation (Barrett and Cooperrider 1990; Barrett, Thomas, and Hocevar 1995; Morgan 1997; Palmer and Dunford 1996). This said realities and relations are constructed in inter-actions that include, but are not confined to, conceptual language. Indeed, one of the ways in which communities (as "forms of life") may differ is in the forms (written, spoken, dance, drumming, etc.) in which relating usually takes place. Indeed, S-O relations may be perpetuated by requiring 'research objects' to inter-act with written texts, for example (see Chapter 3). Being open to, and working with, the many ways in which relating 'goes on' in different communities seems to be an essential orientation. As one illustration, participants can be invited to perform their life story and to re-story it in writing, song, or acting. In so doing, they perhaps learn how to open themselves to new possible ways of 'going on' in relation (Barry 1997). Thus, getting 'unstuck,' learning how to learn, and constructing "power to" go on in new ways become central.

Constructing Eco-Logical Ways of Being

Positive science and its normative ideal of subject-object ways of relating construct realities and relations that are (rationally) instrumentalized, secularized, and dis-embodied (Berman 1981, 1990; Hosking 2008, 2010). Exploring non-S-O inquiry practices involves a shift to eco-logical (rather than ego-logical, self-centered) forms of practice. This means collapsing many of the by now familiar binaries such as secular and spiritual, self and other, and mind and body. In eco-logical ways of relating, 'mind' is extended in the world. Mind is not just embodied in 'our' own body or "flesh" (Lakoff and Johnson 1999); it is extended in the wider ecology of all relational processes. Here we are reminded of Gregory Bateson's (1979) words, "mind is social." We are speaking of a radical departure from the analytic, Anglo-American philosophy to which positive science is so strongly wed. Eco-logical practices accept that action—and what we might think of as feelings, perceptions, and agency—arise from fundamental relatedness and fundamental participation (Bateson 1972; Reason 1994; Gergen 2009b; Shotter 2001). Work of this sort accepts that relating, while it may involve conceptual language, is embodied and sensual action.

As we can see, these orienting themes do not propose specific methods or techniques. Rather, they serve as fluid and flexible resources for action. In the next chapter, we explore the ways in which these resources might re-figure evaluation and assessment. We think it is important to devote a chapter to this topic because inquiries often are used to make decisions about policies, programs, and procedures in education, healthcare, government, business, and daily life. Further, assessment and evaluation have become 'hot topics' now that transparency and accountability are routinely demanded.

Reflection

How do you (or could you) see these themes 'at work' in your own practice (see Table 5.1)?

Table 5.1 Orienting Themes for Transformative Inquiry

Orienting Themes	Your Research
opening space for now-ness	
both knowing and influencing	
unfolding multiple local realities in different but equal relation	
respecting emergent processes and possibilities	
centering appreciation	
embracing both inquiry and intervention	
seeing both questioning and listening as potentially (trans)formative	
constructing in both conceptual and non-conceptual performances	
constructing eco-logical ways of being	

6   Valuing and E/valuation

"It was a queer shaped little creature."

INTRODUCTION

We live in a world obsessed with evaluation. New initiatives and programs are funded or implemented only when there is confidence that they can be evaluated. Existing programs and initiatives can only be sustained if they receive a favorable evaluation. In education, healthcare, government, and business, evaluation and assessment have become not only commonplace but a taken-for-granted form of practice. To evaluate is to do "business as usual."

Our relational discourse invites us to see that the most ordinary aspects of our lives could be seen as evaluative. This is because we are always already participating in a particular set of values and beliefs—"forms of life" where fact and value are inseparable. In addition, because there are multiple, local forms of life, there are also multiple (local) fact/value constructions. We are constantly in the middle of e-valuation and continually poised to e-valuate.

In addition, when it comes to 'methods' of evaluation (when some community-based voice says, 'This is an evaluation'), relational constructionism invites us to reflexively consider the standards of communities and invite participants into collaborative and participatory process of evaluation. We will see that evaluation need not be critical (although it certainly can be). A relational constructionist orientation invites us to adopt an appreciative stance where our appreciation is focused on the value participants give to certain forms of practice and to certain relational realities.

RELATIONAL CONSTRUCTIONISM AND THE INEVITABILITY OF E-VALUATION

We would like to explore evaluation in the context of a relational constructionist discourse. In this context, evaluation is embedded in our ways of talking and acting—in all our inter-actions. Conceptual language plays a very important part in this. Each time we do 'this' or say 'that,' we distinguish among an almost infinite array of possibilities. In other words, language both differentiates and adds some sort of valuation. A simple declaration such as "What a lovely day" distinguishes this view of the day from all other possible views and does so with 'value attached,' so to speak. Our focus on language-based processes points to the (perhaps inescapable) practice of unwittingly and unreflexively passing judgment—of e-valuating. As the poet Robert Graves (1986) remarked, "there's a cool web of language winds us in"; it can seem impossible for us to step outside of language and thus impossible to avoid imposing distinctions and judgments, distinguishing good from bad, better from worse, and so on.

The Danish novelist Peter Hoeg (1994) beautifully captures the ubiquity of judgment in his novel, *Borderliners*, where a troubled teenage boy, boarding at a private school, reflects on the systematic and institutionalized aspects of constant evaluation. Speaking in the boy's voice, Hoeg writes,

> They believed that it was of great help to children to be assessed. I suppose they still believe that. In our society it is a pretty widespread belief. That assessment is a good thing.
>
> I was at the playground with the child . . . she had climbed up on to some railway sleepers. She was about one metre off the ground. She called to me from there. "Look!" I did not get the answer out. I had no time. It came from a stranger—she was also there with her child. "What a clever girl!" she said. I had no time to think. I was on my feet and on my way over to bite her head off. Then I remembered that she was the mother of a small child and that she was a woman. . . . I sat down, but it was a long time before I stopped shaking.
>
> The child had wanted attention. She had just asked to be noticed. But she was given an assessment. "What a clever girl!" (99)

Reflection

Robert Graves (1986), in The Cool Web, *remarked:*

> *"But we have speech to chill the angry day*
> *And speech to dull the rose's cruel scent."*

What do you think he meant by this?

The issue of evaluation strikes us as especially interesting in the context of the commonly voiced critique that relational constructionism is relativist (by abandoning 'real-world' assumptions) and so allows that 'anything goes' (Hosking 2011). Were this true, it would imply that evaluation has no place in a constructionist discourse. However, as we have noted, all aspects of the social world are infused with e-valuation. Relational construction-ism does not imply that the practice of evaluation is wrong or bad. Rather, it invites us to pay attention to the relational practices we engage in when we enter this language game. Are standardized and universalizing ways of determining right and wrong, good and bad, successful and unsuccessful useful to 'going on together' or might there be other ways to relate and evaluate? The relational constructionist premises we have been outlining are centered on 'the how' of constructing relational realities. It is the *process* of evaluation that is our focus—which provides an orientation to prac-tices that are local, situated, and historical in nature. Evaluation *practices* therefore become participatory moments of constructing relational reali-ties; what is valued is reconstructed in process.

When taking a relational constructionist stance, we may participate in the inquiry process in many different ways. Rather than evaluation 'of' others, we prefer relationally engaged practices of evaluation 'with' others (Pearce 1992). This means that we join with participants in some sort of collaborative process. In this process all participants coordinate around issues concerning the forms of practice they value and how they might create more of the same. This requires, of course, that partici-pants explore together what structures of organizations, communities, institutions, and so forth are needed to support valued forms of practice. In other words, we are interested in what might help (perhaps in quite different ways) the various participating forms of life and their orga-nizing activities. To quote Darin Weinberg (2008) on the philosophical foundations of constructionist research, "The practical point of doing constructionist studies has very often been to promote a better way of thinking and, more important, living" (15). But, we should add, in our processual-constructionist orientation, this 'promoting' is viewed as ongoing in the local and continual process of evaluation. In other words, we might refer to outcomes as outcomes-in-process. We should also add that what Weinberg calls "better way(s) of thinking and . . . living" should be locally determined and not assumed to be arrived at via some objective process.

It is important to realize that from a relational constructionist per-spective, evaluation *with* others does not need to start by privileging the form of life or community-based voice of science together with its related assumptions, practices, and interest. This is because we have abandoned the necessity for distinguishing the "context of discovery" and the "con-text of justification" (Chapter 3), thereby placing the voice of science on an equal footing with other community-based discourses. *However, it does not silence the voice of science.* Following from this, some of the new options for action that you might like to consider include working in ways that have the possibility to become more open and multi-logical. This can be contrasted with the mono-logic of the knowing researcher, reflecting the 'logic' (the local rationality) of his or her science community, making decisions about what, how, and why—largely without dialogue—'before' the 'data' collection begins.

Practices that try to facilitate the relational engagement of multiple (community-based) voices include appreciative evaluation and responsive evaluation. Both importantly orient the process of inquiry in ways that attend to the sorts of questions we ask (e.g., problem-oriented questions or questions of value and appreciation) and to the ways in which we are relationally responsive to participants and their local knowledge. These approaches to evaluation may 'go on' in ways that open up spaces for new kinds of conversation and new ways of being in relation, possibilities for multiple local realities (as forms of life, not individual subjectivities) to co-exist as different but equal rather than right or wrong, better or worse in relation to some (claimed) one way things really are.

Given this, it follows that reflexivity is no longer confined to the context of discovery but now extends into the "context of justification" (see Chapter 3). In other words, evaluations are no longer described as the objective outcomes of inquiry but are, instead, considered as "running" or "emerging" texts in relation to other possible narratives. Our constructionist orientation invites us to attend to the particular relational realities constructed, for example, in our scientific writings and theorizing. That is, we attend to the ways in which we position ourselves in relation to the other, for example, through our writing style (formal, distant, neutral).

The same issue arises, for example, in organizational inquiries and interventions and, indeed, in any and all powerful inter-actions as they warrant some realities and not others. In this respect, we see relational processes as both the unit of analysis and the locus of stability and change. One potentially radical implication is that the conventional distinction between evaluation and intervention is unnecessary. All processes, regardless of whether someone calls them evaluation, are now considered actively to construct relational realities.

Of course it is perfectly possible for practitioners to continue to practice 'methods' of evaluation in some sort of subject-object relation and to try to minimize their intrusiveness and effects on others in an attempt to produce relatively objective knowledge about reality. However, as outlined earlier, a relational constructionist discourse sees this as *just one possible way* of constructing realities and relations. Other possible ways include inviting more open, multi-logical approaches.

Reflection

If you are always participating in the norms and values of a particular form of life and inter-acting with other 'forms,'

- *Identify the various forms/communities that are implicated (perhaps at different points) in your practice/inquiry.*
- *How does each e-valuate the ways in which you participate?*
- *If you are planning to write up your inquiry (perhaps for a Ph.D.), by what community-based standards will your text be evaluation?*
- *What could this mean for your inquiry (again, at different stages)?*

EVALUATION AS METHOD

Having spoken about e-valuation as a feature of all relational processes and, so, all inquiry, we now turn our attention to existing practices that use the language of evaluation—to what are often called 'methods' of evaluation. We will begin by saying something about practices that reflect a post-positivist science discourse and go on to speak of those that come closer to some sort of constructionist orientation. Our discussion is intended to highlight differing assumptions and practices so that you can see how they relate to your own 'meta-theory' and to relational constructionism.

Summative Evaluation

This approach, also called end point or product evaluation, has become a popular practice. It makes sense in relation to a positive science discourse. This means that norms and standards within a scientific community are mobilized to determine and measure pre-defined outcomes and related performance. Particular local rationalities dominate—usually those of the funders and contractors. This approach treats evaluation as (1) something to be designed ahead of time; (2) a relatively value-free, objective exercise (where facts are treated as separate from values); (3) separate from the program, intervention, or practice to be assessed; and (4) best achieved through the application of thin (statistics) rather than thick (narrative) descriptors.

Generally, evaluation is seen as a feedback process to funders, practitioners, and (certain) organization members about the progress and impact of some intervention (Cummings and Worley 2001). And, as described previously, evaluation is understood as achieved through scientific research in which the ideal design would consist of measurements pre- and postintervention, a comparison group that does not receive the intervention, and statistical analysis performed by a detached evaluator (Cummings and Worley 2001). In this way, a valid and reliable assessment can be made of differences and whether these are most likely attributable to the intervention; unambiguous answers to these questions can come only from careful, controlled, empirical research (French, Bell, and Zawacki 1994, 327).

So what meta-theoretical assumptions does it put to work? End point, summative, or product evaluation (1) gives an important role to distinctions among ontology, epistemology, and methodology; and (2) attempts to produce objective knowledge about the intervention in relation to (3) some 'technical' (politically neutral, factual) standard on which all rational beings of "cognitive goodwill" could agree (Swanborn 1999). In other words, summative evaluation assumes that, for example, an ability such as learning exists (ontology) and that we can know if such a skill has been achieved (epistemology) by asking the "right" sorts of questions at the "right" time, in particular at the end of a learning module (methodology). This sort of evaluation might assess students after they have engaged in a particular learning experience, and the result of this assessment will indicate whether the experience is effective. In the context of our relational premises, summative evaluation does not aim to be responsive to multiple, local ontologies. It does impose one reality construction (in the name of science and rationality) on others and so reproduces relations of "power over."

Reflection

Have you ever had your work evaluated by such a process?

- *How did it feel?*
- *How useful do you think the results were?*

Responsive Evaluation

For Stake (1975), evaluation is responsive "if it orients more directly to program activities than to program intents; responds to audience requirements for information; and if the different value perspectives present are referred to in reporting the success and failure of the program" (14). This means (1) letting the design emerge during the evaluation process (rather than being pre-determined); (2) including data in the form of thick, textured qualitative material; (3) reporting in a way that maintains diversity (rather than looking for consensus); and (4) giving space for others to make their own judgments based on the data presented.

Turning to his meta-theory, it is clear that Stake views the individual researcher as the one who should be in control of the inquiry. He prioritizes accurate representations (where accuracy is determined by the researcher based on his or her community standards) and distinguishes process and outcome (Hosking and Pluut 2010). So he makes some moves to open up to emergence and multiple voices but continues to center positive science interests and, to that end, a valuing of (some degree of) subject-object relations.

Responsive Evaluation: A Constructivist Variant

An important variant on responsive evaluation can be seen in the work of Guba and Lincoln (1989). They explicitly adopt a "constructivist" methodology, assuming that mind operations construct realities and, consequently, that differences in constructions should be discussed and negotiated to produce "more informed" constructions, to correct "wrong" constructions, and to reach a consensus where possible. They have developed "fourth generation evaluation" and regard it as responsive to the extent that it seeks the views of different stakeholders who determine what questions will be asked and what information will be collected. The multiple reality constructions of different stakeholders are made explicit, confronted, and criticized such that differences can be corrected and negotiated to produce shared conclusions and recommendations. The evaluator's role combines the expertise of the scientist with the tasks of facilitation and of mediation among various stakeholders. Guba and Lincoln stress that evaluation should be disciplined and verifiable, and they devote a great deal of effort to developing methods for assessing its quality.

Responsive Evaluation: A Social Constructionist Variant

Tineka Abma (2000) has developed a version of responsive evaluation that comes closer to our relational constructionist view. A key assumption of her work is that realities are socially constructed in social-relational processes, and multiple social realities are made in multiple social relations. These constructions are no longer viewed as cognitive constructions or as greater or lesser distortions of reality but as local-cultural and constructed 'in word and deed,' so to speak. Given these contexts, her version of responsive evaluation aims to make different constructions explicit and understandable rather than seeking to explain and resolve them.

Abma, in contrast to Stake (1975) and Guba and Lincoln (1989), is concerned with propagating polyphony, appreciating differences, and preserving diversity instead of trying to reduce it. To her, the evaluator lets go of the detached, expert role and subject-object relationship with other. Assumptions are made about multiple forms of expertise located within local knowledge communities. The evaluator works with these to facilitate polyphony; the distinction between the evaluator (researcher) and the evaluated objects (researched) is now more blurred.

In addition and consistent with a relational constructionist perspective, Abma views knowledge as a local-historical construction. For this reason, she finds it important to evaluate a program or an intervention in its own (socio-historical) context, retaining local-contextual details, and focusing on what the locals think to be issues. Thus, she sees storytelling as an important way to conduct the evaluation process—generating evaluative accounts—through social interactions. Consequently, the evaluation report includes stories and dialogues—thick descriptions and multiplicity rather than claiming some narratives as "malconstructions" (Guba and Lincoln 1989) while others are better informed.

Reflection

Perhaps you have participated in such a process, perhaps not. If not, try to imagine your answers to the same questions we asked before:

- *How did it feel (how might it have felt)?*
- *How useful do you think the results were (might be)?*

Heading Toward Relationally Engaged Practices

We now turn to a focus on the resources or potential offered by constructionist discourse. These focus on embracing what people do together. Once more we refer to the novelist Hoeg. The narrator of his story, Peter, devotes most of his time to articulating how standardized tests and evaluations can never get at what is really there. He argues that even in the laboratory, scientists are not measuring the essence of something. And so he advises, "it is important that people enter the laboratory every now and then, and ask questions of a different kind to those that are otherwise asked" (214).

Relational constructionism, by describing subject-object relations as constructions that could be otherwise, allows and invites some very distinctive orientations. We are especially interested in exploring practices that (re)construct soft self-other differentiation—what we have called relationally engaged practices. They seem to involve certain practice orientations: shifting from pathology to potential, entertaining multiplicity, suspending certainty, entertaining possibilities, moving from critique to appreciation, and moving from e-valuation to valuation; we will explore each in turn.

EVALUATION AS A RELATIONALLY ENGAGED PRACTICE

From Pathology to Potential

To get you thinking about this theme and its potential significance, we think it is helpful to point out that when we confront daunting difficulties, we are likely to find ourselves in the hands of professionals. These professionals are charged with the process of assessing those who come seeking help because, as we have mentioned, the traditional discourse of individualism tells us that once we know what is wrong with a person, a community, an organization, or an educational program, we can focus attention on remedial treatments. How do we confront Foucault's (1979) critique of the ways in which disciplinary regimes dis-empower? What about the many deleterious effects such critical evaluative processes have on us (Gergen and McNamee 2000; Kutchins and Kirk 1997)?

Let's briefly examine the institutionalized practices and evaluative context of mental health. There is little way for a person, once stigmatized, to escape. Labels for mental disorder, for example, are notoriously vague; they typically refer to mental tendencies, dispositions, and afflictions not available to public scrutiny (Kutchins and Kirk 1997). And, the professional's "tools" of diagnosis and evaluation make clear to clients that they are not in a position to judge for themselves. The result is that one can never be certain that he or she is ever eventually "free" of the diagnosis. In effect, to be diagnosed in terms of mental disorder, for many, is to embark on a lifetime of existence on the boundary of normalcy. It is to carry forever a sense of self-enfeeblement, self-doubt, incompetence, and general deficiency. This evaluative process can very likely lead to further pathologizing. While evaluation in other contexts (education, organizations) might appear to be less daunting, the process of both self and collective pathology is no different.

In Chapters 4 and 5, we showed that there are other forms of practice that are more collaborative and that open up possibilities rather than close down on problems. An illustration can be found in one doctoral student's proposed research on brain-injured patients. She noted that brain-injured patients are frequently given psychiatric assessments as well as evaluations geared toward day-to-day functioning on a wide range of activities, including social, psychological, physical, and neurological. Ongoing diagnosis is a large part of assessing this population. Diagnosis typically involves a neuropsychologist delivering a battery of tests to the patient. Frequently, spouses or other close family members' assessments are also given serious consideration after extensive interviewing by the professionals. She thought that it might be important to ask whether it is possible to extend the range of relationships participating in this process and simultaneously broaden the assessment or understanding of what counts as quality of life. Ordinarily, quality of life is evaluated by tallying check marks on a list of activities that can or cannot be performed by the patient. Does this standardized measure really tell us about quality of life? Or, better put, who determines quality of life and in what circumstances?

To address these provocative issues, the student designed a process of inquiry that focused on interviewing patients and their families. Her interest was in understanding from within their significant relationships what it meant to have "quality of life." Most of us probably would refer to abstract, cultural standards such as independence in daily activities, including the ability to bathe, dress, and feed oneself. The researcher imagined beginning her interviews by asking the patients themselves to tell a story that captured when they felt most capable and most competent in their relationships with others. Further, following from this story, they were asked to identify what they saw as their own most significant contributions to their quality of life. She hoped this line of exploration would open the possibility for a very different conversation. Her idea was to open dialogue with the patient and significant family members focused on resources rather than deficiencies. Her intention was to explore the resources noted by both patient and family members. To these patients and their families, quality of life might no longer be assessed by applying a set of abstract categories but would be situated in the very parochial arena of their own lives, thereby shifting the conversation from one of pathology to one of potential.

Dialoging Multiple Rationalities

We can see from this illustration that there might be great potential in giving voice to the lived stories of participants. This is beautifully illustrated in the work of the Public Conversation Project (PCP) (Roth et al. 1992) summarized in Chapter 5. As we told you there, Roth and her colleagues engaged people in dialogue on difficult topics such as abortion. They recognized that all strongly held beliefs and positions are located in visceral, lived conversations with others, and yet, in public or professional contexts (such as the handling of foot and mouth) where difficult issues are discussed, personal stories are often de-valued and thought in some way to detract our attention from the "heart of the matter."

Roth and her colleagues found that initiating conversation on difficult issues with a question that invites participants to voice their personal relationship to the issue provides the resources for conflicting groups to engage in dialogue as opposed to debate. What this means is that, rather than engage with another for purposes of proving one's point or "winning the argument," participants harboring opposed orientations take the time to consider the very local rationale or reality of the opposition's stance. As we said in Chapter 5, recognizing that there are multiple and diverse rationalities that gain coherence within different communities is the first step toward transformation.

Returning to our discussion of evaluation, can we imagine listening to the stories of those with whom we work not for purposes of locating those stories within some universalizing evaluative category, but rather for purposes of granting coherence to very diverse views of what is value-able, successful, or unsuccessful? In other words, voicing stories of evaluation can grant a situational coherence to activities that, in another relational context, might be negatively valued. Practices of this sort have the possibility to construct an order of value that is open and full of possibility rather than closed, hierarchical, single-voiced, and judgmental.

Suspending Certainty

As Hoeg (1994) suggests in his novel, *Borderliners*, the certainty with which evaluation proceeds can be extremely debilitating. For us, the challenge could be said to center on how to be a professional and simultaneously suspend what Putnam (1990) called the "God's eye view"—a view from nowhere. Unfortunately, professionalization (which can be seen as a byproduct of modernist attempts to train individuals in the proper methods and techniques required to work in specific fields) has fixed and separated those who "know" and those who are in need of "knowledge" or "being fixed." This can produce daunting expectations—by both clients and professionals. For example, to be a competent and successful consultant seems to require the ability to quickly assess an organization and to generate effective training programs or change initiatives. Other invested parties, such as perhaps government agencies, professional bodies, communities, and corporate headquarters, add further pressures for the consultant to deliver. Jeff, a seasoned business consultant who had worked for 'the big five' and a Ph.D. candidate, remarked, "Certainty in the professional assessment of (in this case) a client organization, is paramount. There is no room for doubt, uncertainty, or for entertaining a myriad of alternatives" (Hicks 2010).

But what would happen if the consultant did entertain alternative possibilities? In order to do so, he or she would need to engage in self-reflexive critique where there is freedom to suspend the certainty that one evaluation, one way of working, one understanding could be the best (or correct). While the consultant has a responsibility to act professionally, for example, in ways that (some community) warrant as competent and ethical, too much certainty reconstructs subject-object relations, separation, and dominance. When we are too certain about our approach, our answers, or our analysis, we close out the voices of others as well as our own polyphony.

Our relational constructionist view calls for reflexive attention to the kinds of relational realities to which we contribute. This includes reflective attention to our practices of inquiry, our transformative development work, evaluation, or, more generally, consulting. We must be constantly asking ourselves which discursive tradition or form of life warrants these particular questions, observations, and conclusions. Why this discourse? Which community is being voiced here and which, by virtue of the ways they are represented, is being erased? This sort of reflexive critique creates what we call relational engagement. A central aspect of reflexive critique is not only the willingness to entertain doubt about our own positions but to give voice to the stories that provide coherence to radically different positions.

Providing conversational arenas where personal narratives can be told and heard with reference to the relational communities within which they are valued also helps participants to avoid over-generalized abstractions.

Dialogue, as a form of evaluation, opens the possibility for multiple voices and possibilities. By entertaining such multiplicity, we are reminded that our own e-valuative beliefs and certainties could be otherwise. Where traditional evaluation assumes that there are metrics that accurately measure or capture what is working in a program or a practice, dialogic e-valuation operates by first creating a context where evaluative conversations take on a different tone. Paramount is that participants feel free to entertain doubt about their own certainty (see Chapter 5). The impulse to determine good or bad, useful or not, with little exploration of the diverse voices participating in the conversation, is transformed into a generative conversation where all involved collaborate in crafting more useful ways of moving forward.

Entertaining Possibilities

As we have noted, evaluation practices often (re)construct worlds of problems and deficiencies—to be fixed or remedied in some way. Some sort of data collection or inquiry (identifying problems) is followed by some intervention or change effort. Distancing, knowing, and influencing (subject-object) relations may predominate. But what if the conversation shifted from charting the history of 'the problem' to the realm of future images? An immediate objection many have is that such a move appears to "ignore" the "very real" problems of persons, organizations, or communities seeking help. Yet the idea here is neither to ignore nor elevate problems as if they were 'how things really are.' After all, our relational constructionist stance focuses on our ways of relating together and notes how these forms of practice construct the worlds we inhabit. To that extent, when we focus our interactions on problems, we live within a problematized reality. And yet many other resources could be generated that could open up other possibilities.[1]

Here we think of Harlene Anderson's (1997) work. When working in a training or supervisory context, Harlene invites participants into an "as if" posture. After a case has been presented, the group participants take turns speaking "as if" they are different members of the client system. Anderson says that by inviting participants to speak "as if" they were the manager or union representative, for example, they engage in a "problem dissolving" process. Here, they are free to voice alternative interpretations of the "problem" and also imagine how else the situation might be. The alternatives, of course, emerge from participants' own local-cultural narratives because their voices are not already steeped in the sedimented and conflicted narrative of the client system. They are free to explore the possibility of other narrations. The co-mingling of multiple voices offers the person presenting the case a symphony of possibilities. Rather than return to the consultation entrenched in problem talk and evaluative/diagnostic truths, the consultant can now enter the conversation with stories that offer images of potential and hope.

Similarly, there are processes where the focus is on imagining an ideal future and the various ways in which a client might real/ize (literally make real) that ideal. What sorts of activities and relationships might the client need to continue? What might be terminated? What could the client begin to develop as possible actions and/or relations? All help to construct the future by acting into it as opposed to acting within what appears to be an already constructed and solidified (problematic) reality.

New efforts of this sort are emerging, each attempting in their own ways to vitalize practical orientations to possibilities rather than pathology. For example, in Chapter 5, we sketched the approach called Appreciative Inquiry (AI) (Cooperrider 1990). Also relevant is the work of Cooperrider and Dutton (1998) on cooperation and global change, performative approaches to psychology (Holzman 1999), articulations of collaborative education (Bruffee 1999; Rogoff, Turkanis, and Bartlett 2001), future searches (Weisbord and Janov 2000), the 'Imagine your city" projects (Browne and Jain 2002), and a host of other projects. These all shift from looking back, diagnosing, and evaluating—deficiency approaches—to a focus on local constructions of what is working and what could be valuable.

The significance of talking about evaluation as a process of social construction is that it allows us to de-essentialize and de-entify (what some construct as) problems. By locating construction in *activities* rather than in people's heads, relational constructionism provides us with alternatives to individualizing and pathologizing.

From Critique to Appreciation

As university professors, we find evaluation to be a necessary aspect of our daily work. When we talked about this with each other, we found that neither of us felt confident in our ability to evaluate our students. Perhaps if we were "true" social scientists we might be able to evaluate our students with greater confidence. As scholars whose work is devoted to articulating a relational constructionist orientation to interaction within a variety of contexts, we do not have the pleasure of embracing the key assumptions of post-positivist approaches to evaluation—acceptable levels of certainty and objectivity—as the basis for action.

Because constructionism embraces knowledge as a relational, community-based achievement rather than a private, individual ability, the entire foundation on which objective evaluation sits is removed. If what we take to be real and true is a local-cultural, local-historical construction, then on what basis can we justify centering only academic community discourses and ourselves as the arbiters when deciding what will count as "right" answers? Isn't the very act of doubting our own ability to independently and (relatively) objectively evaluate our students an enactment of our desire to construct more relationally engaged, multi-voiced, dialogical practices? Below, Sheila describes one evaluative process that she designed and used with many groups of students. We try to show how this mode of evaluation resonates with an appreciative stance and constructionist practices.

As a Visiting Professor in Italy over 25 years ago, I was introduced to the idea of oral exams, a practice not frequently used in evaluating undergraduate students in the US. While this mode of evaluation was daunting to Italian university students, my experience there helped me to revise my own evaluation methods with my American university students. Looking for an alternative to individual evaluations, I developed a variation on the theme of oral examinations. I announced to my students (a practice I would later find less consistent with the collaborative sensibility of constructionism) that they would be participating in an oral evaluation for the course. Their immediate response was fear, understandably. I asked them to have faith and listen to a description of the process. I then told them that they were to select one friend or family member who they would like to invite to participate in a conversation with them about the material we were studying in our course. They could bring anyone they chose to their scheduled exam. I asked them not to "prepare" their guests for the conversation. There would be no specific expectation of their guests beyond their spontaneous participation in conversation during the "exam."

My hope was to meet two objectives: (1) to make an otherwise individual and critical process of evaluation into a relational, generative process where each student, his or her invited guest, and I could appreciate the specific resources developed in our course through a dialogue; and (2) create a context that would require my students to know the abstract, conceptual, and theoretical material we were exploring in the course but be able to articulate it in a manner that was practical, pragmatic, and accessible for anyone.

This process of evaluation was rich. Needless to say, it took hours of my time, but I thoroughly enjoyed it. Students brought their mothers, fathers, siblings, friends, boyfriends, girlfriends, roommates, and co-workers. I would give one short speech after I had been introduced to my students' guests. I would invite our guest to "help" his or her friend or family member by simply participating in conversation. If the guest wanted to expand on what he or she understood the student to be explaining, he or she should feel free. If the guest felt that the student was not being clear, he or she should say so. I asked our guests to avoid trying to "make the student look good" for the evaluation and explained that any attempt to let the student use obtuse language without translating into common vernacular would, in fact, probably not be helpful to the student. My aim was to encourage our guests to collaborate with the student in a conversation where knowledge would be crafted jointly. Obtuse or abstract language would clearly miss the mark of dialogue and turn quickly into a monologue.

In order to evaluate each student's performance during his or her "oral exam," I invited each person present (myself, the student, and the guest) to summarize the hour-long discussion by commenting on what we all learned, what the highlights of the conversation were to each of us, and what we each would like to develop further if we could have a second conversation. This was part of my attempted shift to appreciation rather than critique. Not only did my students walk away from this process feeling that there was at least one thing they could do really well, as a byproduct of participating in our course, but they left having someone else in their life—outside of our class—with whom they could continue the conversation. Someone significant was now grappling with the implications of individualist and relational ideologies. There was someone to talk with in a way that would value and appreciate the collaborative and transformative nature of our daily lives.

The story's end must be about the ultimate evaluation: grades. Of course this process of relational and appreciative evaluation had to be eventually translated into the language of the institution. Yet, engaging in a dialogic process like this one creates not only a new process for evaluation but, with that process, a new meaning for what it means to give and receive grades.

Reflection

In your own professional context, how might you design a similar dialogic evaluation process?

From Evaluation to Valuation

Annual or biannual evaluations and performance reviews are an unquestioned part of organizational life. To most of us, these rituals of evaluation are not only regular and expected; they are required. How else can we know if the organization is making good decisions and moving in useful directions or if its employees are effectively and efficiently contributing to the organization's mission? If we were to do away with evaluation in our organizations, we believe we would threaten our ability to compete in the local, national, and global markets. Our need to "know" who is good and who is useless and what service is working well is amazingly powerful when we chart the day-to-day operations of the organization.

It is difficult to imagine a world where evaluation is dismissed. Our need to know who and what is pushing our organization ahead has become vital information. Yet, evaluation processes are typically focused on the competencies or incompetencies of individuals. Even an organization's attempt to consider working relationships in the evaluation process (i.e., working teams, departments, levels of management, etc.) generates an aggregate of the individual members of the particular relational unit being reviewed. The challenge we confront is how to move the review and evaluation processes away from an individual focus on deficiencies and flaws and toward generative appreciation of what is meaningful and useful in the organization.

Here we see that not only do multiple inter-relations become central but so too does the move from evaluation to valuation. Evaluation is, as we have said, a question of value. What does the organization value in and of its members? What do different groups or "forms of life" (administration, different groups of professionals, clients) value about the organization and about each other? When we ask these questions, the process of evaluation begins to shift to a relational rather than an individual focus. Consider the variety of relationships that have a stake in crafting an organization's mission: the field or trade of the organization, other like organizations, the local context within which the organization resides, the local and global markets with which the organization must do business, the members of the organization, and their families. With so many voices, the valuations of different forms of life (what some call stakeholders) are likely to be diverse.

SOME CONCLUDING COMMENTS ON EVALUATION

The term evaluation means "the action of appraising or valuing, a . . . statement of value . . . the action of evaluating or determining the value" (*Oxford English Dictionary* 2010). We have said something about how it could be possible to transform individually focused practices of evaluation to relationally oriented *processes of valuation*. Let's now try to summarize the main themes:

- To the constructionist, language is a differentiating device, and thus e-valuation is an inevitable part of relating as what we talk about becomes "this" and not "that" and makes a major contribution to the relational realities we (re)construct and inhabit.
- Recognizing this allows us to engage in ways that "hold lightly" any particular form of differentiating and open up to alternative possibilities.
- This makes evaluation a complex, polyvocal activity grounded in multiple local, historical, situated forms of practice.
- Thus, evaluation is viewed as a form of engagement.
- This invites us to reflect on the forms of engagement that might be useful in helping participants continue to create generative practices. We propose:
  - centering relational processes, not individuals,
  - including multiple local rationalities,

- generating participatory practices,
- orienting toward desired futures, and
- emphasizing and coordinating strengths, abilities, and passions.

In the next chapter, we explore issues of quality and ethics—two issues that have traditionally been bound to the notion of universality. The challenge is to explore how a relational constructionist stance avoids rampant relativism while simultaneously embracing the possibility for multiple and often diverse constructions of quality and ethics.

7 Quality
Reflexivity, Dialogue, and Relational Aesth-et(h)ics or So What?

"Could you tell me please, which way I ought to go from here?"

QUALITY

Let us begin by sharing our conversations with each other about the aim and scope of this final chapter. We began with the working title of "quality." Our aim was to talk about how we might explore (judge?) the "soundness" and utility of any process of inquiry (any research)—after all we have said that 'not anything goes.' Who decides what counts as good research, on what basis, and on what criteria? The issue of quality seemed appropriate for inclusion in this text, and, indeed, we felt it to be an important area to discuss. However, we soon found ourselves being pulled toward engaging with the traditional positive science concerns of reliability and validity. Of course we concentrated on the various attempts to develop revisions that seemed more consistent with our relational constructionist discourse (Denzin 2008; Kvale 2008). But, as we struggled, we realized that this was not what we wanted to do either. At one point we abandoned the term "quality" altogether. We continued to write, taking seriously our feeling that we wanted to write about reflexivity and ethics, and those were the appropriate topics. We wanted to go beyond the realm of evaluation (discussed in the last chapter) and to underscore the very unique understanding of reflexivity and ethics suggested by a relational constructionist discourse.

But somehow the term "quality" remained lurking in the background. Quality felt as though it could and should embrace the kinds of concerns toward which we were feeling pulled. In other words, we felt that the term "quality" addressed our belief that our actions serve as invitations into moral orders (just as they emerge out of local moral orders) and thus they serve as ethical possibilities, the "quality" of which are endlessly unfolding. Trusting in this, we began to explore some of the ways in which quality has been defined to see if we could find something that resonated with us and, more particularly, with our very special sense of relational ethics. Of course the most usual discourse assumed entities with characteristics (qualia) together with related distinctions, for example, between fact and value, objective and subjective knowledge. Work of this sort embraces views of quality as a factual property and views that focus on (what the theorist constructs as) subjective valuations of usefulness and aesthetics. In other words, this work embraces what we earlier (see Chapter 3) called entitative theorizing or what Sampson (1993) called bounded or possessive individualism.

And then, there are ways of talking about ethics that embrace much of the relational stance we are proposing here but do not seem to take it far enough. As illustrations we can point to the work of Levinas (1985) and Buber (1971). Both argue for a view of ethics that is coherent in part with a relational constructionist stance. Yet, there are significant departures. Both focus on the relational nature of human interchange. Levinas talks about ethics as a "first philosophy" from which knowledge emerges (a second philosophy), thereby reversing the philosophical trend that places knowledge as the first philosophy from which ethics emerge. The idea that knowledge emerges from relational, ethical practice is wholly consistent with our argument here. Similarly, Buber features I-Thou relations over I-It relations, thereby acknowledging the central importance of relationality. So, while both orientations recognize the significance of self and other in making meaningful worlds (i.e., ethical worlds), they do so from the starting point of the bounded individual. Thus, it is the individual actor who "recognizes" his or her interdependence on the "other." Perhaps we can say that Levinas and Buber made important strides toward a relational understanding of human interaction, but they did not go far enough. For both, the locus of all meaning is still within the phenomenal world of an acting subject.

In contrast, our relational constructionist discourse invites us to see quality as constructed in relational processes and so differently constructed by different communities in relation to their own local norms, values, and interests. When it comes to our own practices as consultants, researchers, and change workers, we have clearly indicated that we lean toward 'relationally engaged' practices, toward soft self-other differentiation. In this context, we want to highlight three interrelated themes that can be thought of in terms of quality: (1) reflexive practices, which include examining our own ways of entering into the process of inquiry; (2) dialogue and ecological ways of being in relation; and (3) what might be called the ethical and aesthetic aspects of construction.

Reflection

This is really about value. Indeed, there are some forms of practice—some forms of life—that we prefer over others. Relational constructionism is not an "anything goes" orientation.

- *So, how do we simultaneously articulate our preferred life forms and not claim them as True, Real, Right, or Universally better?*
- *How might you hold on to your preferences without imposing them (oppressively) on others?*

RELATIONAL CONSTRUCTIONISM,
REFLEXIVITY, AND HELPING

Relational constructionism centers the processes in which person, world, and their relations are constructed. Practices that refer to—and have their meaning in relation to—a relational constructionist discourse embrace the view that they simultaneously reflect and, in the process of inquiry, actually re-construct the orienting premises and interests. In other words, and as we remarked in Chapter 3, this is very obviously inquiry "with philosophy" (Bentz and Shapiro 1998). As we examine the world, we change it. In so doing, we change our understanding of what we know (ontology), how we know it (epistemology), and how we might (re)produce it (methodology).

Reflexivity

Reflexivity is often presented as a unique characteristic of science. Its scope is usually restricted to the design, procedure, and outcomes of scientific inquiry, or, to put it another way, its scope typically is restricted to the context of discovery. Put otherwise, reflexivity in positive science is focused on assessing the quality of the knowledge *produced by* (i.e., discovered by) the research design and practices. But, as we saw in Chapter 3, our relational constructionist perspective does not require that the contexts of discovery and justification be held apart. This means that the scope of reflexive practices can include paying attention to the scientist's or inquirer's discourse (critical realism, relational constructionism, etc.) and the possibilities it opens up/closes down in the (inquiry) processes of constructing self, other, and relations; for us, this is crucial.

We are quite happy to extend reflexivity to include the relational constructionist discourse itself. This is because we need no "protective veil" to separate the discourse from the empirical world so that we can legitimately test its ability to generate (probable) truths. Nor are we interested in developing content-rich theoretical frameworks about, for example, leadership, organization, or conflict management. Rather, we are interested-in— indeed we are passionately oriented toward—*the practical potential* of the relational constructionist discourse as it is put to work in particular (local-cultural, local-historical) cases. So, put very broadly, our interest is in the *possible worlds* that are (not) opened up, the 'new' ways of being in relation that can (not) emerge, and how helpful these are to the different local forms of life that are implicated. *This is the context of our reflexive concerns*, not the more usual one of examining the quality of our knowledge claims and possible sources of error.

We are very aware that once again we have set our relational constructionist discourse apart from other meta-theoretical constructions. Indeed, as practitioners of relational constructionism, we seem to be abandoning differentiations that other communities find useful. We want to emphasize that it is not our intention to be nihilistic or to claim some higher ground from which we can look down, so to speak, on other discourses/practices. We want to stress that while particular differentiations (e.g., of fact and value, real and good) may be common, they are by no means common to all communities and all times (back to our comments about cultural-historical shifts), and they necessarily exist in relation to other possible constructions.

One of the differentiations we have softened is the distinction between scientific inquiry and inquiry performed in the context of other forms of life. As we said in Chapter 1, it is possible to think of all persons engaging in inquiry—and not just as scientists. Inquiry can be thought of as being open and curious and taking a reflective orientation toward our own practices and judgments. Indeed, we guess that many of you are reading this book because you have a reflexive interest in your own professional practice and/or in your chosen research topics. As we saw earlier, perhaps relational constructionism can provide you with a way of thinking—with an orientation to your own practice as teacher, consultant, or manager—that can open up "new voyages of discovery" and new possible worlds (Harding 1998).

Practical Know How

Here we think again of some of the professionals and students with whom we work and, for example, the inquiries they are pursuing. Some very explicitly articulate their interest in the practical usefulness of their reflective inquiries. In what follows, we offer a brief text from a former Ph.D. student, Jeff. His work seems to provide a marvelous illustration of the practical utility of reflective inquiry. For more than twenty years, Jeff worked as a director, as a senior manager in business strategy for PricewaterhouseCoopers, and as a Managing Consultant in IBM Business Consulting Services. Relational constructionism, reflexivity, and a passionate interest in helping have become central to his thesis and his preferred approach to consulting. Some time after Jeff began working with Dian Marie, he wrote this concept paper to tell how he imagined his Ph.D. thesis.

Jeff: On the purpose and motivating influences of this thesis
I want to be helping. I want to be helping clients and business consultants. I want to be helping clients and business consultants address organizational issues and problems. I want to be helping clients and business consultants address organizational issues and problems by developing and explicating a relational constructionist alternative to the prevailing and modernist-influenced 'expert approach' to management consulting.

I begin with purpose—what I want to be doing—as a way of introducing the themes and the writers that motivate and influence the writing of this thesis. From Richard Rorty and pragmatism comes the primacy of purpose, and usefulness as a guide for action. The purpose is to be help-ing, guided by the needs of clients and consultants in practice, as they are, for example, addressing organizational issues and problems. Another motivation/influence is from Wittgenstein and the performative, genera-tive function of language, as opposed to a representative or descriptive function. Thus, this thesis is not intended to be primarily *about* consult-ing and how to help client and consultants; rather, it is intended *to be helping them.* A third motivation/influence is from Heidegger and the idea of being in the world. This is not an attempt to construct an a-tem-poral, for-all-time approach to consulting. The purpose is to be help*ing* as business consulting confronts the limitations of modernist-influenced ideals of professionalism and of organizations, similar to the challenges faced and dealt with in varying ways and to varying degrees by other professions, including medicine, psychology, and public planning. Also from Heidegger is the notion that people are as they are doing, and that we may better understand ourselves and those around us more fully and usefully by asking not '*Who* are you?' but rather '*When* are you?' I 'am' most when I am helping others address their organizational issues and problems, least constrained by: pre-conceived roles; pre-conceived bod-ies of knowledge; an overriding concern for accurate representation of a single, timeless truth; set interpretations of past, present or future; or entitative power. Social construction provides useful guidance on how realities emerge. Relational constructionism brings the focus closer to clients and consultants in particular, to how we might 'get along' better together in addressing issues and problems. The focus is not on expli-cating the attributes of 'the client-consultant relationship,' as some*thing* that exists between self-contained individuals, but rather on developing a more full and useful understanding of—as well as the possibilities of—'clients and consultants relating' or 'clients and consultants in rela-tion.' (Hicks 2010)

Jeff used the language of "helping" to talk about his research and his driving interest, purpose, and passion. But he is not talking about helping as an instrumental relation between subject and object. This is not talk of helping 'from the outside,' by a fully formed, self-existing, knowing, and structuring subject in relation to a self-existing, ready-to-be-known, and shaped object. Helping in the context of our relational construction-ist perspective implies some sort of recognition of (an)other as intimately connected with (a)self. In this context, helping refers to some sort of turn-ing toward and opening up to other. As we have seen in earlier chapters, this means orienting ourselves (in consulting, inquiring, or 'intervening') in ways that are open to other(ness), for example, through working with minimal structures, listening and being relationally responsive, improvis-ing, opening multiple dialogues, appreciating rather than judging, and not being too quick to know. Returning to our earlier reflections on Western individualism, this orientation de-centers The Self and "celebrates the other" (Sampson 1993).

Reflection

It is interesting to reflect on what inspires us to do the work we do. How is it that we come to select particular professions, particular topics of study, and particular communities with which to work? We find it useful to explore these questions. They help us situate ourselves within our own inquiry processes. We suggest you answer the following questions at frequent intervals throughout your inquiry process:

- *What draws me to this topic, this community, this way of working?*
- *What do I imagine might happen as a result of this work?*
- *What might others imagine could happen?*
- *How might I be changed by this work?*

DIALOGUE, ECO-LOGICAL WAYS OF BEING, AND PRACTICAL WISDOM

We have spoken at length about dialogue in connection with our constructionist or "dialogical" view of person and our orientation to consulting, inquiry/research, and/or change-work. We have suggested that dialogue, when viewed as a special kind of talk, seems key to opening up to other(ness). Dialogue is grounded in the assumption of interrelatedness—we might call this a relational ontology—self and other are seen as inextricably interrelated. Some speak of this as the assumption of a "participative ontology," whereas others speak of an "eco-logical" (rather than "ego-logical") view of personhood (Bateson 1972; Hosking 2000). For us, these are all ways of speaking about letting go of subject-object constructions and opening up to relationally engaged practices that invite and allow 'the outside' in, so to speak. As we remarked in Chapter 5, dialogical practices include surrendering, suspending our usual constructions of what is 'real and good,' appreciating rather than e-valuating, and opening up to ongoing-ness or what Bohm spoke of as flow. In dialogue, "all presumptions of the true, the rational, and the good are open to suspicion"; dialogue can provide the space in which "new realities and practices are fashioned" (Gergen 1994, 62–3).

In the following, we give another example of some consulting work in which helping, relational engagement, discursive practices, and dialogue stand central.

Dian Marie: Creating a Buddhist-inspired hospice

A little over a year ago, Bettine (a consultant doing her Ph.D. with me) told me that she was talking with someone called Ernst about a project he had initiated to create a Buddhist-inspired hospice for end-of-life care. He needed help with various issues of management and organization. She wanted to help and she knew I would too. The three of us met together a number of times, slowly getting to know one another, cooking and eating together, sharing stories from our different backgrounds and expertise. Over a period of months the three of us identified a cluster of interrelated research/development projects (background research on other hospices and their practices, developing a website, etc.), found people who were keen to take them on, and got the projects up and running.

During the course of these conversations and activities, I learned that to make the hospice happen, Ernst had given up his job, had created a legal entity, and had raised some initial funding. Two volunteers had joined him to create a management board, and a lot was happening. In our ongoing meetings, I learned that he was feeling stuck. Our conversations slowly shifted and came increasingly to focus on the organizing processes by which Ernst was attempting to create the hospice. As I recall, I repeated an earlier proposal (which hadn't been taken up—I think it had not been heard) to have one of our development projects focus on these very processes. And so Ernst and I began what turned out to be a series of meetings in which he would reflect on his experiences, I would make connections with relational constructionism, and we would explore links with Shambhala Buddhism.[1] We also wrote and exchanged notes.

Ernst expressed great appreciation for how much he was learning (not without some pain when it came to reflections on particular events and decisions) from 'my expertise.' He wrote, "My practice, together with our conversations, are helping me to reflect on what I can learn from the process so far and how to go on from here." I expressed and felt great appreciation for the opportunity to have these conversations and to experience how relevant and helpful Ernst found them.

We continued to meet regularly; I continued to explore with Ernst how it could be possible to organize in ways that we have here called soft self-other differentiation—ways that Buddhism describes as open, compassionate, and being in the now. During this time Ernst significantly changed the ways he went about bringing the hospice to fruition. Members of his first management board resigned, and Ernst took his time creating a new board, waiting until he was confident that those who came to volunteer their help had a strong commitment to the hospice and to particular ways of working. Our development projects then had the space to work as semi-autonomous working groups. We had meetings to share progress and ideas, and dialogical practices became central to our ways of working, as did regular reflections on how we were going on together. (Kleisterlee and Hosking 2009)

Some time after these events, we came across the book, *Synchronicity* (Jaworski and Flowers 1998), in which the authors write about Jaworski's experiences of creating a leadership institute. Jaworski's story also seems to illustrate connections among reflexivity, dialogical practices, and the relational view. The authors tell of Jaworski's shock when his wife asked for a divorce. Things 'fell apart,' so to speak. This led him to seriously reflect on his life and the person he had become. He describes many "arresting moments" (Shotter and Katz 1999) associated, for example, with heading off without a plan to places he didn't know and becoming more and more open to whatever came his way. He began a journal, writing about his feelings and experiences, writing about books and conversations that struck him. His journal was a reflective dialogue with himself and with others.

He wrote about experiencing a shift from felt separation (seeing himself and other as independent existences) to fundamental relatedness (we would say to a "relational" or ecological construction). This shift included a growing desire and commitment to serve something beyond himself. This took the form of deciding to create a leadership institute that was oriented toward servant leadership, which meant serving with compassion and heart. He made a leap of confidence, so to speak. He left his job and gave himself up to creating the Institute.

After 'the leap' came the void—what he called "a domain without maps." There he fell into what he spoke of as "traps," which were his previous patterns, his "old ways of being." The first of these was "the trap of responsibility," seeing himself as indispensable, as responsible for everyone and everything. This placed all focus on him rather than what he called "the larger calling." He called his second trap "the trap of dependency"— feeling dependent on a few key staff, key funders, and so on. He was not as straightforward as he should have been, and he did not speak from his center. He wrote of having reverted to "focusing rigidly on the business plan . . . instead of focusing on the result, the vision we had intended" (Jaworski and Flowers 1998, 125). He stopped being flexible, stopped listening, and became more fearful.

The third trap Jaworski called the "trap of over-activity." This came from having people in the organization who were not "aligned with the dream . . . resulting in deep incoherence in the organization" (127). Jaworski and Flowers (1998) wrote, "In these situations, it's not 'they' who are responsible. It's us. It has to do with our own history" (129). Getting out of this trap requires *individual and collective reflection*: "Unless we have the individual and collective discipline to stay anchored, we will eventually lose the flow" (129). He further wrote that at some point he came across Bohm's work on dialogue and had the strong feeling of "that's it!" He was struck by what Bohm said—this was what he knew, and these were the practices that he had gradually come to realize were essential—from his own experiences. Jaworsky had learned *"the discipline of dialogue."* He had learned how essential it is for an eco-logical way of being, fundamentally interrelated with, rather than separating from other and otherness.

The practices we have been describing could also be spoken of in terms of *know-how-in-action* knowing rather than knowledge. This interest in helping—rather than in theory development, testing, prediction, and control—reminds us of Toulmin and Gustavsen's (1996) description of their kind of action research. They noted that it was "aimed at practical effects not theoretical rigor . . . ," which they, in turn, linked to "the kind of knowledge Aristotle called phronesis ('practical wisdom') more than episteme ('theoretical grasp')" (xx).

What we see in the stories of Ernst and Jaworski is a stepping into the moment with others. Both stories share in the movement away from imposing expertise or searching for the 'right' knowledge or method. Instead, Ernst and Jaworski centered their activities on being relationally engaged. This attentiveness to what others understand as 'help,' coupled with a very pragmatic, practical focus on what-'we'-are-doing-together-in-this-context-now, shifts us into the domain of ethical action. We are invited to reflect on what counts as ethical practice within a relational constructionist stance. It is to this that we now turn.

Reflection

As you reflect on your own inquiry process, what challenges or "traps" have you encountered? How did you engage reflexive practice to pull yourself out of these traps?

- *How did you manage the "trap of responsibility?"*
- *How did you manage the "trap of dependency?"*
- *How did you manage the "trap of over-activity?"*
- *In what ways did you embrace "knowing-how-in-action?"*
- *What were some of the "arresting moments" that helped you hold on to an eco-logical way of being?*

THE ETHICS AND AESTHETICS OF RELATIONAL PRACTICE

Ethics

In the discourse of positive science, quality issues arise in relation to the (scientist's) desired separation of subject and object and how thoroughly this is achieved. Issues of ethics are separated from issues dealing with the production of objective knowledge; this is one aspect of the separation of fact and value discussed earlier. As a result, ethical concerns tend to be constructed in terms of trying to avoid unfortunate byproducts. You could say that the focus is on how *not to* intervene in the lives of the researched.

So, for example, this might be attempted through following a professional code of conduct, by guaranteeing anonymity of participants, by having adequate debriefs after 'data collection,' and so on. Professional practice is often guided and assessed through 'before and after' ethical audits (e.g., by some auditing committee of scientists). Another way to make this point is to say that the production of knowledge is viewed as an issue of quality, and ethics is seen as more a matter of a necessary, desirable condition.

In contrast, relational constructionism—by not assuming the necessary separation of knowledge and influence, inquiry and intervention, fact and value, self and other—both broadens the scope of ethics and gives what might be called ethical or moral issues a central place in our inquiries.

Relational constructionism invites a reconstructed and expanded notion of ethics that centers the entire inquiry process. Key to this is the assumption of local relational realities as different "forms of life" with their own language games and local rationalities (what is constructed as real and good—in 'word and deed') (see Chapter 3). Relational processes then are viewed as processes of (re)constructing local rationalities and relations with other "forms of life." Or, put otherwise, ethics concerns the relational processes at play when diverse forms of life are coordinated, requiring something beyond a dominance of one set of values and beliefs over the other. Perhaps we could describe relational ethics as a process of coordinating multiplicity in an attempt to keep the conversation going. If our realities are created in what we do together, then continuing our engagements (or our "doings" with each other) opens the possibility for continued and ongoing coordination and meaning-making.

This raises questions about the forms of life that are invited and supported, excluded or perhaps suppressed in any human science inquiry as well as in community or organizational interventions. The interest in multiplicity (or its apparent absence) and relations (e.g., different but equal—relational constructionism—or dominant—positive science) *can be seen as an ethical interest*. Sheila has written about this as a matter of *relational responsibility* (McNamee 2004d; McNamee and Gergen 1999). But now, the responsibility is for *the process* and the kinds of people and worlds it (re)produces; to be relationally responsible (ethical) is to be attentive to the very process of relating itself. For us, a potential (ethical and practical) interest becomes one of opening up (rather than closing down) possibilities and an orientation to change from 'within' (transformation) rather than from 'the outside.' To return to the theme of subject-object relations and alternatives, we see relational ethics as a stance for constructing 'soft' rather than "hard" self-other differentiation (see Chapter 3).

We imagine that those of you reading this volume are practitioners who engage in inquiry as a common practice. We also imagine that those with whom you work—your clients—view you as experts. You are positioned (Davies and Harre 1990) as being well versed in the subject of your investigation. However, your clients are also experts. Granted, the expertise is of a different kind. As we have discussed before, this raises the question of whose form of life (if any) should be privileged in our inquiries. Why should only one local-communal rationality dominate? Both inquirer and those inquired about (researcher and researched) contribute to the realities that are constructed, and consequently both inquirer and those inquired about intervene in each other's lives.

If we think about the process of inquiry in terms of stories we tell *in cooperation and coordination with others*, then it becomes relevant to consider how these multiple perspectives/multiple stories are able to co-exist in different but equal relation. Some of the coordinating community-based voices might include the people or groups with whom we are working (the people and groups we "study" in traditional terminology), the voices of our colleagues who critique and evaluate our work and who also influence how we engage in our inquiry, and the voices of the broader communities in which we live that also inform our decisions about what questions are important, to name only a few. The questions we ask are always situated within complex webs of relatedness.

Reflection

At this point, it might be useful to consider once again the multiple communities involved in your inquiry. The following are some questions that might begin to open up consideration on the diverse and perhaps competing moral orders at play. Of course, consideration of these diverse communities has important implications for the ethics of your work.

- *Who is involved in your inquiry?*
- *Is this a community that has invited this inquiry?*
- *Who is most interested in this inquiry project?*
- *How will this work affect you?*
- *Who might be the "invisible" participants in this inquiry?*
- *Who will be or could be the audience for the emergent "outcome" of this inquiry?*

A story from Sheila

At a conference on relational practices, a family therapist told his story of working with poor families in a slum of Mexico City. He had deliberately selected this poor community in hope of working collaboratively to improve conditions for families—and particularly for young people. Yet, his initial attempt to offer therapeutic services was thwarted; he quickly learned that families living in the ghetto rarely seek therapy. He was in no position to impose his services on the community; he could not force troubled youth, for example, to seek counseling. He understood that he was an outsider.

Thus, in an attempt to engage families, he moved his own family into the neighborhood. He quickly found that just being in the same community, the same context, was not enough. Still, despite all the problems and difficulties families faced day in and day out (drugs, alcohol, violence, death), and despite his constant presence and availability, the families did not rely on his services. His attempts to call open meetings were acknowledged with a resounding silence and lack of engagement.

One consistent aspect of this community that the therapist quickly recognized was, unfortunately, the ritual of the wake after a community member's death. Since almost all the youth in the community were associated with gangs, and since these gangs were constantly at war with one another over turf, drugs, etc., shootings, deaths, and inevitably wakes were almost a weekly event. And they were community-wide events. As this therapist described the ritual, all members of the community would come and sit for hours at a time in a large circle, sometimes quietly chatting with each other. This group would include families who affiliated with warring gangs, and yet, in the context of the wake, all members were united. Despite day-to-day differences, there was a sense of community that emerged through death in this community.

The therapist attended each wake just as his neighbors did, and, recognizing that the wake was where families and community members gathered, he asked one evening if the group gathered would be interested in having a conversation about life in the community and the problems confronted by all. The participants happily agreed to talk about these issues. This spawned a series of active involvements in transformative projects throughout the community—all addressing the issues that would likely, in another community, bring individuals, couples, and families to psychotherapy. Metaphorically, in this community, death was transformed into new life potentials.

In our view, this therapist's eventual mode of collaborating with community members embodies an ethic of relational inquiry, which is a recognition and respect for local practices. His story illustrates for us the benefit of suspending our certainty as professionals. By questioning the utility of meeting clients in the psychotherapy context as well as questioning the utility of identifying individuals or families as the treatment unit, this therapist was able to join in a fully participatory mode of social transformation. He was probably less likely than most to identify himself as the professional who was helping people change. We are sure he was more inclined to talk about the mutual transformations for himself, his family, members of this community, and the therapeutic process as well.

Reflexive dialogues, such as the one into which this therapist invited community members, can make the process of inquiry a 'becoming process,' in which The Researcher (practitioner) becomes someone who contributes *one (community-based) expertise among many*. Dian Marie's story of her reflective dialogues with Ernst is also relevant here as are other examples such as participative action research and some of the approaches to evaluation outlined in Chapter 6. As was suggested by Hardy, Phillips, and Clegg (2001; also see Latour 1987), researchers (inquirers) would do well to encourage reflexive dialogues about the narratives participants draw on and the local constructions they mobilize. So, a 'researcher' (practitioner, professional) could try to generate new ways of relating by exploring *other participants'* interests in participating, inviting them into dialogues of equals, to co-create responsibility for the process.

These issues are illustrative of a relationally sensitive ethic. Our relational constructionist discourse provides no foundational truths to be impressed and imposed on others and no grand theories to cover all particularities. Instead, we see theories as byproducts of relational interchange, and, in this sense, theories themselves are both (more or less) practical and ethical; they point toward certain pragmatic ways of being, and each of these resources for action has ethical implications. This does not mean that we are left with rampant relativism. As we discussed earlier, within any discursive community (i.e., within any local ontology) there are constraints; we are not free to act however we want. Our ways of talking and acting gain relevance, sustainability, and viability only when others supplement our actions in particular ways. This implies that we can no longer impose our ethics (our way of talking, of acting) on others. Doing so fails to acknowledge that a significant change in one's actions demands that the interactive moment provide the participants with the means by which alternative interactive resources may be called on—conditions that do not often apply in research, consultation, or social change processes.

As practitioners we can attempt to provide such opportunities by understanding our practices as discursive moments that are part of the shifting yet "real" (in the local and relational sense) relational realities that participants co-construct. Given our relational dialogic perspective, we might shift from questions such as, "Why is X the case?" and "What causes X?" to "How do I come to identify X as the topic of investigation?" or "How do I come to 'know' that X is the case?" This is a relational—not an essentializing—question because the answer requires that the practitioner tell how, *in conversation with others*, these 'objects of study' were given meaning and life. Similarly, we might ask, "How is it that what people *do* together provides the opportunity for particular descriptions to emerge and remain viable?" This question creates a context where a multiplicity of voices can co-mingle. It places an emphasis on reflective dialogues, voiced and unvoiced. Significant questions include: Who is this inquiry/research for? Who *could* it be for? How many different stories could be told? How might others frame the central questions? How might others design the inquiry process (e.g., research method)?

When language-based relational processes provide the starting point, there is no*thing* to discover or explain but rather different ways of relating in which to engage. Inquiry, as a form of professional practice, is one way of talking/acting. We co-construct realities with the people and groups we 'study,' 'consult,' 'teach,' and 'treat' when we engage in inquiry. Those realities are part of the web of relations in which both professional practitioner and client (in traditional terminology: researcher and researched) participate. This sensitivity to relational practice *is* an ethic of practice.

It should be apparent by now that a relational constructionist stance toward inquiry is not oriented toward providing instructive answers to questions such as: How can we determine what is (usually) right or good or appropriate? To answer that question requires moving beyond the nuanced details of any particular situation. Yet, doing so ignores the very particular processes by which people come to understand their specific situation. When people hear us speak about dialogic potentials for coordinating diverse worldviews, they immediately toss a "hot issue" our way: What about gay marriage? What about terrorism? What about the Israeli/Palestinian divide? How would you determine a resolution to these conflicts? Our answer is always: We don't know, specifically. But we do know that a shift in how we *approach* the focus of our inquiry can be transformative, and a new approach requires juggling complex and varying worldviews, not simplifying them.

We have tried to emphasize that our talk of "relating" includes humans *and the wider phenomenal world to* implicate any-one or any-thing we relate to as 'there,' as 'that,' as not self. Our talk of relating has also emphasized relationally engaged ways of 'going on.' We repeat this again now in order to point out that this considerably broadens the landscape of quality and ethics when compared with positive science. As we suggested earlier, our emphasis on eco-logical (rather than ego-logical) ways of relating calls forth a practical-moral or ethical interest in issues such as climate change, environmental devastation, loss of species and habitats, starvation in the Sudan, and so on. This interest includes paying attention to the futures that might be given our actions in the here and now. Our work is not focused on creating new knowledge but on making livable futures—or, in the words of Wittgenstein (1953), finding how to "go on together."

Aesth-et(h)ics

We hope that it is by now clear that our constructionist orientation diverts us from looking for an absolute 'Truth.' This raises the question of how we are to speak and write about our work when we are not speaking or writing from the traditional persuasive mode of the expert who can document the basis of their truth claims. It seems to us that this sort of writing and talking requires a 'light touch.' We like to employ stylistic practices that depart from the dogmatic mode of expert talk (the scientist, the professional, etc.)

and, instead, embrace the notion of possibility or provocation. Our style of presentation should be inviting and open-ended. Rather than claims to truth, we strive to offer invitations into generative potentials. The distinction we are addressing might be best captured in the move from 'this is how it is' to 'this is how it might be.'

Styles of writing and talking typically draw on rhetorics that privilege claims to truth, evidence, facts, and objectivity. The task for the constructionist is not to critique this style as wrong but rather to move beyond this right/wrong style to a form of presentation that invites the other (the reader or the listener) into conversation. Finding ways to perform this aesth-et(h)ic style is one of the most challenging aspects of our work. It is here, in our writing, in our speaking, and in our performance, that the coherence of relational constructionism is generated. If we adopt relational constructionism as a philosophical stance, then our job is to put it into practice in everyday interactions as we operate within our professional and personal domains. This means that our writing and speaking 'about' relational constructionism cannot be just that. We are not talking and writing *about* a particular inquiry technique or strategy. We are, instead, *performing* inquiry. We are living and acting and being relational in our everyday engagements. For many, this is the most challenging aspect of a relational constructionist stance. It is not enough to talk/write about it. We must perform it.

The above has connections with Aristotle's distinction between poiesis and praxis. Poiesis is purposive, rational action with instrumental aims. Praxis, in contrast, is action where there is no goal to produce a specific product but to realize (literally, make real) some moral order. Praxis is not a neutral technique or method for producing 'good' or 'right.' Instead, praxis is an inherent part of what is accomplished; it is a form of 'doing action.' In praxis, it is impossible to separate process from product. Praxis relies on phronesis (what Aristotle called practical wisdom)—the sort of wisdom that unfolds in the interactive moment.

If we focus on inquiry as praxis, how can we hold on to our passion for our work and avoid presenting that work dogmatically? Rhodes and Brown (2005) had something to say on the matter in their discussion of the process of writing responsibly. They offered five themes that could help relational constructionist researchers move away from explanation toward opening space for what might be possible. First, they suggest that we view our writing (and, by implication, our speaking) as a creative act, thereby blurring the distinction between fact and fiction. As they say, "It may be that borrowing from literary genres can assist us in our efforts to produce more interesting and readable accounts" (483). Second, they encourage us to be vulnerable, just as those who participate in our inquiry are positioned. "It is no longer acceptable for us to ask others to reveal something of themselves while we 'remain invulnerable' " (483).

Third, we are urged to recognize that our inquiry is not only an inquiry into the lives and practices of those we study, but it is also—and very much the case—an inquiry into our "uniquely personal 'voice' " (484). Fourth, they encourage us to write (and speak) in a style that is accessible to the multiple communities connected with our research process. Rhodes and Brown remind us that we must assume the responsibility of engaging our multiple audiences and that, in so doing, we "enlarge their moral sympathies" (484). And finally, we must acknowledge that when we write or speak as professionals, our words and actions are far from neutral (as science is presumed to be). We are invested with disciplinary power (Foucault 1980) often beyond our understanding. The 'presentation' of our inquiry and the meaning generated in that presentation is not only a relational achievement but a rhetorical one as well. Reflexive questioning focused on what sort of world we are inviting others into when we speak or write in particular ways is a necessary aspect of relational constructionist inquiry.

To present the 'results' of our inquiry in ways that are coherent with a relational constructionist stance requires us to perform in different ways. We avoid dogmatic, right/wrong language. We position ourselves in such a way that alternative understandings may be considered. We can do this with the words we choose (e.g., "It was discovered" vs. "Within this particularly community, we noticed"), the form of presentation we employ (standard research report written exclusively for other experts or scholars vs. personal narrative, music, drama, etc.), and the venues we use for sharing our work (professional journal vs. community blog).

We do not mean to suggest that traditional scholarly or professional forms of expression are off limits. Rather, we hope to expand the array of audiences we reach and the spectrum of voices we might use in communicating the processes of our inquiries. Our challenge is to think about how we might speak to multiple audiences either simultaneously or by exploring diverse venues and media. The question we must ask is, *who do we want to know about what we are constructing with this community?*

Reflection

Following Rhodes and Brown's suggestions, consider the following in terms of your own inquiry processes:

- *Are you writing, talking, and performing as if you have discovered the "facts" or are you inspiring your audiences to imagine, to step into a world of possibilities?*
- *Do you feel vulnerable as those participating in your inquiry might? What vulnerabilities have you encountered?*
- *In what ways is this inquiry an inquiry into your own identity?*
- *Who are you writing/speaking to as you describe your inquiry?*
- *What sort of world are you inviting others into with your work?*

TOWARD TRANSFORMATIVE INQUIRY

Did we have a purpose for this chapter and have we fulfilled it? When Dian Marie was newly graduated, she worked for the Engineering Industry Training Board (EITB) in the UK as a researcher. Her immediate boss, Don Bates, gave her some very helpful lessons in writing. He would say, "You have to tell them, 'What do we know, how do we know it, and so what?'" We hope to have said something about the 'so what' in this chapter. It turned out to be an exciting journey—working out what we did and did not want to address. It turned out to have the quality of, in some sense, already known—a process of re-discovering what we had to say, which reminded us of T. S. Eliot's (1968) line, "And know the place for the first time."

Recommended Reading

INTERVIEWING

Gubrium, Jaber F., and James A. Holstein, eds. 2003. *Postmodern interviewing*. London: Sage.

Holstein, James A., and Jaber F. Gubrium. 1995. *The active interview*. London: Sage.

Jovchelovitch, Sandra, and Martin W. Bauer. 2000. Narrative interviewing. In *Qualitative researching with text, image and sound: A practical handbook*, edited by Martin W. Bauer and George Gaskell. London: Sage.

Kvale, Steinar, and Svend Brinkman. 2009. *InterViews: Learning the craft of qualitative research interviewing*. London: Sage.

ETHNOGRAPHY (INCLUDING AUTO-ETHNOGRAPHY, NARRATIVE, AND COLLABORATIVE)

Ellis, Carolyn, and Arthur P. Bochner, eds. 1996. *Composing ethnography: Alternative forms of qualitative writing*. Walnut Creek, CA: AltaMira Press.

Goodall, H. Lloyd. 2000. *Writing the new ethnography*. Lanham, MD: Rowman and Littlefield.

Goodall, H. Lloyd. 2008. *Writing qualitative inquiry: Self, stories, and academic life*. Walnut Creek, CA: Left Coast Press.

Hammersley, Martin. and Paul Atkinson. 2007. *Ethnography: Principles in practice*, 3rd edition. New York: Routledge.

Holstein, James A., and Jaber F. Gubrium. 2008. Constructionist impulses in ethnographic fieldwork. In *Handbook of constructionist research*, edited by James A. Holstein and Jaber F. Gubrium. New York: Guilford Press.

Kondo, Dorinne. 1990. *Crafting selves: Power, gender and discourses of identity in a Japanese workplace*. Chicago: University of Chicago Press.

Lassiter, Luke E. 2005. Collaborative ethnography and public anthropology. *Current Anthropology* 46:83–106.

Lather, Patti. 2001. Postmodernism, post-structuralism and post(critical) ethnography: Of ruins, aporias and angels. In *Handbook of ethnography*, edited by Paul Atkinson, Amanda Coffey, Sara Delamont, John Lofland, and Lyn Lofland. London: Sage.

Madison, D. Soyini. 2005. *Critical ethnography: Methods, ethics, and performance*. London: Sage Publications.

Thomas, Jim. 1991. *Doing critical ethnography*. Newbury, CA: Sage.

NARRATIVE, DISCOURSE, AND DISCOURSE ANALYSIS

Andrews, Molly, Corinne Squire, and Maria Tsamboukou, eds. 2008. *Doing narrative research*. London: Sage.

Barry, David. 1997. Telling changes: From narrative family therapy to organizational change and development. *Journal of Organizational Change Management* 10 (1):30–46.

Boje, David M. 2001. *Narrative methods for organizational and communication research*. London: Sage.

Center for narrative research (CNR). Available at http://www.uel.ac.uk/cnr/index.htm

Czarniawaska-Joerges, Barbara. 1996. *Narrating the organization: Dramas of institutional identity*. Chicago: Chicago University Press.

Gee, James Paul. 2005. *An introduction to discourse analysis, theory and method*. New York: Routledge.

Gee, James Paul, and Michael Handford, eds. 2011. *Routledge handbook of discourse analysis*. London: Routledge.

Hepburn, Alexa, and Sally Wiggins, eds. 2007. *Discursive research in practice*. Cambridge, UK: Cambridge University Press.

Holstein James A., and Jaber F. Gubrium. 2011. *Varieties of narrative analysis*. London: Sage.

McLeod, John. 1997. *Narrative and psychotherapy*. London: Sage.

Potter, Jonathan, and Alexa Hepburn. 2008. Discursive constructionism. In *Handbook of constructionist research*, edited by James A. Holstein and Jaber F. Gubrium, 275–293. New York: Guilford.

Ramsey, Caroline M. 2005a. Narrating development: Professional practice emerging within stories. *Action Research* 3 (3):279–295.

Ramsey, Caroline M. 2005b. Narrative: From learning in reflection to learning in performance. *Management Learning* 36 (2):219–235.

Rhodes, Carl, and Andrew Brown. 2005. Narrative, organizations and research. *International Journal of Management Reviews* 7 (3):167–188.

Sarbin, Theodore R., ed. 1986. *Narrative psychology: The storied nature of human conduct*. New York: Praeger.

Watson, T. 2009. Narrative, life story and manager identity: A case study in autobiographical identity work. *Human Relations* 62 (3):425–452.

ACTION RESEARCH, APPRECIATIVE INQUIRY, AND RELATIONAL/PARTICIPATIVE APPROACHES

Katz, Arlene M., Loring Conant, Jr., Thomas S. Inui, David Baron, and David Bor. 2000. A council of elders: Creating a multi-voiced dialogue in a community of care. *Social Science & Medicine* 50 (6):851–860.

McNiff, Jean, and Jack Whitehead. 2006. *All you need to know about action research*. London: Sage.

Preskill, Hallie, and Tessie Tzavaras Catsambas. 2006. *Reframing evaluation through appreciative inquiry*. London: Sage.

Reason, Peter. 1998. *Human inquiry in action: Developments in new paradigm research*. London: Sage.

Reason, Peter, and Helen Bradbury, eds. 2001. *Handbook of action research: Participative inquiry and practice*. London: Sage.

Shotter, John. 2009. Situated dialogic action research: Disclosing 'beginnings' for innovative change in organizations. *Organizational Research Methods* 13:268–285.

Stayaert, Chris, and Bart van Looy, eds. 2010. *Relational practices, participative organizing*. Bingley, UK: Emerald.
Watkins, Jane M., and Bernard Mohr. 2001. *Appreciative Inquiry: Change at the speed of imagination*. San Francisco: Jossey-Bass/Pfeiffer.

QUALITY, RELIABILITY, VALIDITY, AND TRUSTWORTHINESS

Kvale, Steiner. 2002. The social construction of validity. In *The qualitative inquiry reader*, edited by Norman Denzin and Yvonne Lincoln. London: Sage.
McNamee, Sheila. 1994. Research as relationally situated activity: Ethical implications. *Journal of Feminist Family Therapy* 6 (3):69–83.
Rhodes, Carl, and Andrew Brown. 2005. Writing responsibly: Narrative fiction and organization. *Organization* 12 (4):467–491.
Salmon, P. 2003. How do we recognize good research? *The Psychologist* 16 (1):24–27.

REFLEXIVITY, ETHICS, AND LOCAL USEFULNESS

Alvesson, Matts, and Kai Skoldberg. 2000. *Reflexive methodology: New vistas for qualitative research*. London: Sage.
Chia, Robert. 1996. *Organizational analysis as deconstructive practice*. Berlin: De Gruyter. Cunliffe, Ann L. 2002. Critical pedagogy: Reflexive dialogical practice in management learning. *Management Learning* 33 (1):35–61.
Cunliffe, Ann L. 2003. Reflexive inquiry in organizational research: Questions and possibilities. *Human Relations* 56 (8):983–1003.
Hardy, Cynthia, and Stewart Clegg. 1997. Relativity without relativism: Reflexivity in post-paradigm organization studies. *British Journal of Management Studies* 8:5–17.
Hardy, Cynthia, Nelson Phillips, and Stewart Clegg. 2001. Reflexivity in organization and management theory: A study of the production of the research subject. *Human Relations* 54 (5): 531–560.
Haynes, Kathryn. 2006. A therapeutic journey? Reflections on the effects of research on researcher and participants. *Qualitative Research in Organizations and Management: An International Journal* 1:204–221.
Johnson, Phil, and Joanne Duberley. 2003. Reflexivity in management research. *Journal of Management Studies* 40:1279–1303.
Steier, Fred. 1991. *Research and reflexivity*. London: Sage.
Woolgar, Steve, ed. 1988. *Knowledge and reflexivity: New frontiers in the sociology of knowledge*. London: Sage.

PARADIGMS, PARADIGM ISSUES, AND MULTI-PARADIGM RESEARCH

Bem, Sacha, and Huib Looren de Jong. 2006. *Theoretical issues in psychology*, 2nd ed. London: Sage.
Benton, Ted, and Ian Craib. 2001. *Philosophy of social science*. Basinsgtoke, UK: Palgrave.
Chia, Robert, and B. MacKay. 2007. Post-processual challenges for the emerging strategy-as-practice perspective: Discovering strategy in the logic of practice. *Human Relations* 60:217.

Cunliffe, Ann. L. 2010. Crafting research: Morgan and Smircich 30 years on. *Organizational Research Methods*. Online First.

Deetz, Stan. 1996. Describing differences in approaches to organization science: Rethinking Burrell and Morgan and their legacy. *Organization Science* 7 (2):195–207.

Edwards, Derek, M. Ashmore, and Jonathan Potter. 1995. Death and furniture: The rhetoric, politics and theology of bottom line arguments against relativism. *History of the Human Sciences* 8:25–49.

Kvale, Steinar, ed. 1992. *Psychology and postmodernism*. London: Sage.

Harding, Sandra, and Merrill Hintikka, eds. 1983. *Discovering reality: Feminist perspectives on epistemology, metaphysics, methodology and philosophy of science*. Dordrecht: Reidel.

Lewis, Marianne, and Mihaela Kelemen. 2002. Multi-paradigm inquiry: Exploring organizational pluralism and paradox. *Human Relations* 55 (2):271–275.

Manicas, Peter T., and Paul Secord. 1983, April. Implications for psychology of the new philosophy of science. *American Psychologist*, pp. 399–413.

Slife, Brent, and Richard Williams. 1995. *What's behind the research? Discovering hidden assumptions in the behavioural sciences*. Thousand Oaks, CA: Sage.

SOME RELATED DISCUSSIONS OF AND ORIENTATIONS TO INQUIRY

Alvesson, Matts, and Stanley Deetz. 2000. *Doing Critical Management Research*. London: Sage.

Bentz, Valerie Malhotra, and Jeremy J. Shapiro. 1998. *Mindful inquiry in social research*. Thousand Oaks, CA: Sage.

Denzin, Norman K., and Yvonna S. Lincoln, eds. 2005. *The Sage handbook of qualitative research*. London: Sage.

Flyvbjerg, Bengt. 2001. *Making social science matter: Why social inquiry fails and how it can succeed again*. Cambridge, UK: Cambridge University Press.

Gergen, Mary, and Kenneth Gergen. 2003. Qualitative inquiry. Tensions and transformations. In *The landscape of qualitative research*, edited by Norman Denzin and Yvonne Lincoln. Newbury Park, CA: Sage.

Holstein, James A., and Jaber F. Gubrium, eds. 2010. *Handbook of constructionist research*. New York: Guilford.

Hunt, Celia, and Fiona Sampson. 2005. *Writing: Self and reflexivity*. Basingstoke, UK: Palgrave Macmillan.

Law, John. 2004. *After method: Mess in social science research*. Abingdon: Routledge.

Lightburn, Anita, and Phebe Sessions, eds. 2005. *Handbook of community-based clinical practice*. New York: Oxford University Press.

Prushi, Prasad. 2005. *Crafting qualitative research: Working in the post-positivist traditions*. Armonk, NY: Sharpe.

Richardson, L. 2003. Writing: A method of inquiry. In *Collecting and interpreting qualitative materials*, edited by Norman Denzin & Yvonne S. Lincoln, 499–541. London: Sage.

Wilson, S. 2008. *Research is ceremony: Indigenous research methods*. Winnipeg: Fernwood Publishing.

Wright, Thomas A. 2006. Toward the development of a truly relational approach to the study of organizational behaviours: Further consideration of the committed-to-participant research perspective. In *Relational perspectives in organizational studies*, edited by Olympia Kyrikidou and Mustafa Ozbilgin. Cheltenham, UK: Edward Elgar.

POSTMODERNISM, ORGANIZATION, AND INQUIRY

Boje, David, Robert Gephart, and Tojo Thatchenkery, eds. 1996. *Postmodern management and organization theory*. London: Sage.

Chia, Robert. 1995. From modern to postmodern organizational analysis. *Organization Studies* 16 (4):579–604.

Chia, Robert. 1996. *Organizational analysis as deconstructive practice*. Berlin: Walter de Gruyter.

Cooper, Robert, and Gibson Burrell. 1988. Modernism, postmodernism and organizational analysis: An introduction. *Organization Studies* 9 (1):91–112.

Hassard, John, and Martin Parker, eds. 1993. *Postmodernism and organizations*. London: Sage.

Kilduff, Martin, and Ajay Mehra. 1997. Postmodernism and organizational research. *Academy of Management Review* 22 (2):453–481.

Newton, Tim. 1996. Postmodernism and action. *Organization* 3 (1):7–29.

Taylor, Bryan C. 2005. Postmodern theory. In *Engaging organizational communication theory and research*, edited by Steve May and Dennis Mumby. Thousand Oaks, CA: Sage.

WORKS ON SOCIAL CONSTRUCTIONISM

Burr, Vivian. 2003. *Social constructionism*, 2nd ed. London: Routledge.

Cunliffe, Ann L. 2002. Social poetics: A dialogical approach to management inquiry. *Journal of Management Inquiry* 11:128–146.

Cunliffe, Ann L. 2008. Orientations to social constructionism: Relationally-responsive social constructionism and its implications for knowledge and learning. *Management Learning* 39:123–139.

Dachler, H. Peter, and Dian Marie Hosking. 1995. The primacy of relations in socially constructing organizational realities. In *Management and organization: Relational alternatives to individualism*, edited by Dian Marie Hosking, H. Peter Dachler, and Kenneth. J. Gergen, 1–29. Aldershot, UK: Avebury.

Danziger, Kurt. 1997. The varieties of social construction. *Theory and Psychology* 7 (3):399–416.

Gergen, Kenneth J. (2009). *Relational being: Beyond self and community*. Oxford, UK: Oxford University Press.

Hosking, Dian Marie, H. Peter Dachler, and Kenneth J. Gergen, eds. 1995. *Management and organization: Relational alternatives to individualism*. Aldershot, UK: Avebury.

Lock, Andy, and Tom Strong. 2010. *Social constructionism: Sources and stirrings in theory and practice*. Cambridge, UK: Cambridge University Press.

McNamee, Sheila, and Kenneth J. Gergen, eds. 1992. *Therapy as social construction*. London: Sage.

McNamee, Sheila, and Kenneth J. Gergen. 1999. *Relational responsibility: Resources for sustainable dialogue*. Thousand Oak, CA: Sage.

Parker, Ian, ed. 1998. *Social constructionism, discourse and realism*. London: Sage.

Pearce, W. Barnett. 1992. A 'camper's' guide to constructionisms. *Human Systems: The Journal of Systemic Consultation & Management* 3:139–161.

Pearce, W. Barnett. 2007. *Making social worlds: A communication perspective*. Malden, MA: Blackwell.

Shotter, John. 2010. *Social construction on the edge: 'Withness' thinking and embodiment*. Chagrin Falls, OH: Taos Institute Publications.

EVALUATION RESEARCH

Abma, Tineka. 2005. Responsive evaluation in health promotion: Its value for ambiguous contexts. *Health Promotion International* 20 (4):91–397.

McNamee, Sheila. 2006. Appreciative evaluation in an educational context: Inviting conversations of assessment and development. In *The social construction of organization*, edited by Dian Marie Hosking and Sheila McNamee. Copenhagen: Liber.

Patton, Michael. 2002. *Qualitative research and evaluation methods*. London: Sage.

Preskill, Hallie, and Tessie Tzavaras Catsambas. 2006. *Reframing evaluation through appreciative inquiry*. London: Sage.

van der Haar, Dorieke, and Dian Marie Hosking. 2004. Evaluating appreciative inquiry: A relational constructionist perspective. *Human Relations* 57 (8):1017–1036.

Wadsworth, Yolanda. 1997. *Everyday evaluation on the run*. London: Allen & Unwin.

JOURNALS

British Journal of Social Psychology
Human Relations
Journal of Management Inquiry
Management Learning
Organization
Organization Studies
Qualitative Inquiry
Qualitative Research Journal
Organisational Research Methods
Systemic Practice and Action Research
The Journal of Applied Behavioural Science

WEBSITES

Discourse Unit Publications: http://www.discourseunit.com/publications_pages/publications_books.htm

Participatory Studies: http://participatorystudies.com

New Economics: http://www.neweconomics.org/ (see e.g., work on participatory approaches)

Peter Reason/participatory action research: http://www.peterreason.eu/

Dian Marie Hosking's website: www.relational-constructionism.org

The Taos Institute: http://www.taosinstitute.net

The Qualitative Report: http://www.nova.edu/ssss/QR/index.html

Appreciative Inquiry Commons: http://appreciativeinquiry.case.edu/

Sheila McNamee's website: http://pubpages.unh.edu/~smcnamee/

Notes

NOTES TO CHAPTER 2

1. It is interesting to note the ways in which the terms "proof" and "certainty" still dominate both professional and lay contexts.
2. In addition, the active-passive dichotomy appears in many local theories such as theories of leadership and organizational design where, for example, the organization—follower or team member—is conceptualized as a passive object that can be known and re-formed by the active leader or change agent. It has also been linked to constructions of gender and to gendered versions of science.
3. Theories of leadership, for example, position organizational leaders and leaders of task groups as those who can and must build their individual knowledge of other who is tacitly assumed to stay still long enough for them to do so. Similarly, end-point evaluation studies are assumed to find out "how it is" as the basis for subsequent intervention through power over other.
4. Similarly, theories of organizational design often position strategic management and consultants as those who can achieve "power over" the organization by rationally manipulating its characteristics to match its environment.

NOTES TO CHAPTER 3

1. Given the recent dominance of this modernist discourse in the Western world, many of you might be asking, "So, what's the problem?" Because we live within language communities, we rarely find ourselves in disagreement that the word "chair" refers to an object on which we sit. Yet, what does the word "justice" or "loyalty" mean? And, in fact, what does "chair" mean when the object referred to is used to barricade a door or when uttered in a culture where people sit only on floor cushions?
2. We would add that we include other, not just as other people but also what commonly is storied as non-sentient objects (landscapes, trees, technology, etc.) as discussed earlier.

NOTES TO CHAPTER 6

1. Here we think of work that focuses on metaphors and shifting from (locally) unhelpful metaphors to more helpful ones; see, for example, the work on "generative metaphor intervention" (Barrett and Cooperrider 1990; Barrett, Thomas, and Hocevar 1995).

NOTES TO CHAPTER 7

1. We had both been active in the Shambhala Buddhist community (in different sanga) for more than ten years.

Bibliography

Abma, Tineke. 1996. *Responsive evaluation*. Delft: Eburon.

Abma, Tineke. 2000. Fostering learning-in-organizing through narration: Questioning myths and stimulating multiplicity in two performing art schools. *European Journal of Work and Organizational Psychology* 9 (2):211–231.

Alvesson, Matts, and Stanley Deetz. 2000. *Doing critical management research*. London: Sage Publications.

Anderson, Harlene. 1997. *Conversation, language, and possibilities: A postmodern approach to therapy*. New York: Basic Books.

Anderson, Harlene, and Diane R. Gehart. 2007. *Collaborative therapy: Relationships and conversations that make a difference*. New York: Routledge.

Anderson-Wallace, Murrey, Chris Blantern, and Tom Boydell. 2001. Advances in cross boundary practice: Inter-logics as method. *Career Development International* 6 (7):414–420.

Argyris, Chris, Robert Putnam, and Diana McLain Smith. 1985. *Action science*. San Francisco: Jossey-Bass.

Argyris, Chris, and Donald A. Schön. 1974. *Theory in practice: Increasing professional effectiveness*, 1st ed. San Francisco: Jossey-Bass.

Argyris, Chris, and Donald A. Schön. 1978. *Organizational learning*, Vol. 2, *Addison-Wesley OD series*. Reading, MA: Addison-Wesley.

Bakhtin, M. M. 1981. *The dialogic imagination: four essays*. (M. Holquist, Ed., C. Emerson and M. Holquist, Trans.).Austin: University of Texas Press.

Bakhtin, M. M. 1986. *Speech genres and other late essays*, 1st ed., (V.W. McGee, Trans.). *University of Texas Press Slavic series*. Austin: University of Texas Press.

Barrett, Frank. 2006. Living in organizations: Lessons from jazz improvisation. In *The social construction of organization*, edited by D. M. Hosking and S. McNamee. Malmo, Sweden: Liber.

Barrett, Frank, and David Cooperrider. 1990. Generative metaphor intervention: A new approach for working with systems divided by conflict and caught in defensive perception. *Journal of Behavioural Science* 26 (2):219–239.

Barrett, Frank, Gail F. Thomas, and Susan P Hocevar. 1995. The central role of discourse in large scale change: A social construction perspective. *Journal of Applied Behavioral Science* 31 (3):352–372.

Barry, David. 1997. Telling changes: From narrative family therapy to organizational change and development. *Journal of Organizational Change Management* 10 (1):30–37.

Bateson, Gregory. 1972. *Steps to an ecology of mind*. New York: Bantam.

Bateson, Gregory. 1979. *Mind and nature: A necessary unity*. New York: E. P. Dutton.

Bem, Sacha, and Huib Looren de Jong. 2006. *Theoretical issues in psychology.* London: Sage.

Benton, Ted, and Craib, Ian. 2001. *Philosophy of social science.* Basingstoke, UK: Palgrave.

Bentz, Valerie Malhotra, and Jeremy J. Shapiro. 1998. *Mindful inquiry in social research.* Thousand Oaks, CA: Sage Publications.

Berger, Peter, and Thomas Luckmann. 1966. *The social construction of reality: A treatise in the sociology of knowledge.* New York: Doubleday.

Berman, Morris. 1981. *The re-enchantment of the world.* Ithaca, NY: Cornell University Press.

Berman, Morris. 1990. *Coming to our senses.* New York: Bantam Books.

Bohm, David, Donald Factor, and Peter Garrett. 1991. Dialogue: A proposal. http://www.infed.org/archives/e-texts/bohm_dialogue.htm.

Bohm, David. 2004. *On dialogue.* (Lee Nichol, Ed.). New York: Routledge.

Boje, David M. 1995. Stories of the storytelling organization: A postmodern analysis of Disney as "Tamara-Land." *Academy of Management Review* 38 (4):997–1035.

Boje, David M. 2001. *Narrative methods for organizational and communication research.* London: Sage Publications.

Bowker, G., and Bruno Latour. 1987. A booming discipline short of discipline— (Social) studies of science in France. *Social Studies of Science* 17 (4):715–748.

Browne, Bliss W., and S. Jain. 2002. *Imagine Chicago: Ten years of imagination in action.* Chicago: Imagine Chicago.

Bruffee, Kenneth A. 1999. *Collaborative learning: Higher education, interdependence, and the authority of knowledge,* 2nd ed. Baltimore, MD: Johns Hopkins University Press.

Buber, Martin. 1971. *I and thou.* New York: Free Press. Original edition, 1937.

Buber, Martin, Maurice S. Friedman, and Ronald Gregor Smith. 1965. *The knowledge of man: Selected essays.* New York: Harper and Row.

Bunker, Barbara B., and Billie T Alban. 1997. *Large group interventions: Engaging the whole system for rapid change.* San Francisco: Jossey-Bass.

Burr, Vivien. 2003. *Social constructionism.* East Sussex: Routledge.

Calas, Marta B., and Linda Smircich. 1991. Voicing seduction to silence leadership. *Organization Studies* 12 (4):567–602.

Carspecken, Phil F. 1996. *Critical ethnography in educational research: A theoretical and practical guide.* New York: Routledge.

Ceglowski, D. 2001. Research as relationship. In *The qualitative inquiry reader,* edited by N. K. Denzin and Y. S. Lincoln. London: Sage Publications.

Chambers, Robert. 1994. The origins and practice of participatory rural appraisal. *World Development* 22 (7):953–969.

Chasin, Richard, and Margaret Herzig. 1992. Creating systemic interventions for the sociopolitical arena. In *The global family therapist: Integrating the personal, professional, and political,* edited by B. Berger-Could and D. H. DeMuth. Needham, MA: Allyn & Bacon.

Chasin, Richard, Margaret Herzig, Sallyann Roth, Laura Chasin, and Carol Becker. 1996. From diatribe to dialogue on divisive public issues: Approaches drawn from family therapy. *Mediation Quarterly* 13 (4):323–344.

Chia, Robert. 1995. From modern to postmodern organizational analysis. *Organization Studies* 16 (4):579–604.

Chia, Robert. 1996. The problem of reflexivity in organizational research: Towards a postmodern science of organization. *Organization* 3 (1):31–59.

Chia, Robert. 2003. Organization theory as postmodern science. In *The Oxford handbook of organization theory,* edited by H. T. A. C. Knudsen. Oxford, UK: Oxford University Press.

Chia, Robert, and S. Morgan. 1996. Educating the philosopher manager: De-signing the times. *Management Learning* 27 (1):37–64.

Conquergood, Dwight. 1997. Street literacy. In *Handbook of research on teaching literacy through the communicative and visual arts*, edited by J. Flood, S. B. Heath, and D. Lapp. New York: Macmillan.

Cooperrider, David. 1990. Positive image, positive action: The affirmative basis of organizing. In *Appreciative management and leadership: The power of positive thought and action in organizations*, edited by S. Srivastva and D. Cooperrider. San Francisco: Jossey-Bass.

Cooperrider, David, and Jane Dutton. 1998. *No limits to cooperation: The organization dimensions of global change.* Newbury Park, CA: Sage Publications.

Cooperrider, David, and Suresh Srivastva. 1987. Appreciative inquiry into organizational life. In *Research into organizational change and development*, edited by R. W. Woodman and W. A. Pasmore. Amsterdam: Elsevier.

Corradi Fiumara, Gemma. 1990. *The other side of language: A philosophy of listening.* London: Routledge.

Cottor, Robert, Alan Asher, Judith Levin, and Cindy Caplan Weiser. 2004. *Experiential learning exercises in social construction.* Chagrin Falls, OH: Taos Institute Publications.

Cronen, V. E., K. M. Johnson, and J. W. Lannamann. 1982. Paradoxes, double binds, and reflexive loops: An alternative theoretical perspective. *Family Process* 21 (1):91–112.

Crowther, David, and Dian Marie Hosking. 2005. Accounting in Bable? Constructing social accounting as a multi-logical performance. *Critical Perspectives on Accounting* 16:535–550.

Culler, J. 1982. *On deconstruction: Theory and criticism after structuralism.* Ithaca, NY: Cornell University Press.

Cummings, Thomas, and Christopher G. Worley. 2001. *Essentials of organization development and change.* Cincinnati, OH: South-Western College Publishing.

Cunliffe, Anne. 2010. Crafting qualitative research: Morgan and Smircich 30 years on. *Organizational Research Methods* 13 (1):1–27.

Cushman, Philip. 1995. *Constructing the self, constructing America: A cultural history of psychotherapy.* Boston, MA: Addison-Wesley.

Czarniawska, Barbara. 2001. Narrative, interviews, and organizations. In *Handbook of interview research: Context and method*, edited by J. F. Gubrium and J. A. Holstein. Thousand Oaks, CA: Sage Publications.

Czarniawska, Barbara. 2008. *A theory of organizing.* Cheltenham, UK: Edward Elgar Publishing Limited.

Czarniawska-Joerges, Barbara. 1997. *Narrating the organization: Dramas of institutional identity.* Chicago: University of Chicago Press.

Dachler, H. Peter, and Dian Marie Hosking. 1995. The primacy of relations in socially constructing organizational realities. In *Management and organization: Relational alternatives to individualism*, edited by Dian Marie Hosking, H. Peter Dachler, and Kenneth J. Gergen. Aldershot, UK: Avebury.

Danziger, Kurt. 1997. *Naming the mind: How psychology found its language.* London: Sage Publications.

Davies, Bronwyn, and Rom Harre. 1990. Positioning: The discursive production of selves. *Journal for the Theory of Social Behaviour* 20 (1):43–63.

Deetz, Stanley. 1996. Describing differences in approaches to organization science: Rethinking Burrell and Morgan and their legacy. *Organization Science* 7 (2):191–207.

Denzin, Norman K. 2008. *Qualitative inquiry and the politics of evidence.* Walnut Creek, CA: Left Coast Press.

Edwards, Derek, and Jonathan Potter. 1992. *Discursive psychology, inquiries in social construction.* London: Sage Publications.

Eliot, T. S. 1968. *Four quartets.* Boston: Mariner.

Ellis, Carolyn. 2004. *The ethnographic I: A methodological novel about autoethnography.* Walnut Creek, CA: AltaMira Press.

Fairclough, Norman. 1989. *Language and power.* New York: Longman.

Fals-Borda, Orlando, and Mohammed Anisur Rahman. 1991. *Action and knowledge: Breaking the monopoly with participatory action research.* New York: Apex Press.

Fawcett, S. B., A. Paine Andrews, V. T. Francisco, J. A. Schultz, K. P. Richter, R. K. Lewis, E. L. Williams, K. J. Harris, J. Y. Berkley, J. L. Fisher, and C. M. Lopez. 1995. Using empowerment theory in collaborative partnerships for community health and development. *American Journal of Community Psychology* 23 (5):677–697.

Fine, Michelle. 1994. Working the hyphens: Reinventing self and other in qualitative research. In *Handbook of qualitative research,* edited by Norman Denzin and Yvonne Lincoln. London: Sage Publications.

Fleck, Ludwik. 1979. *Genesis and development of a scientific fact.* Chicago: University of Chicago Press.

Foster, E., and A. P. Bochner. 2008. Social constructionist perspectives in communication research. In *Handbook of constructionist research,* edited by J. A. Holstein and J. F. Gubrium. New York: Guilford.

Foucault, Michel. 1972. *The archaeology of knowledge.* London: Tavistock Publications.

Foucault, Michel. 1979. *Discipline and punish: The birth of the prison.* New York: Vintage Books.

Foucault, Michel. 1980. *Power/knowledge: Selected interviews and other writings, 1972–1977.* New York: Pantheon Books.

Fox, Karen V. 1996. Silent voices: A subversive reading of child sexual abuse. In *Composing ethnography,* edited by E. Ellis and A. P. Bochner. Walnut Creek, CA: AltaMira Press.

French, Wendell L., Cecil Bell, and Robert A. Zawacki. 1994. *Organization development and transformation: Managing effective change.* Burr Ridge, IL: Irwin.

Gergen, Kenneth J. 1991. *The saturated self: Dilemmas of identity in contemporary life.* New York: Basic Books.

Gergen, Kenneth J. 1994. *Realities and relationships: Soundings in social construction.* Cambridge, MA: Harvard University Press.

Gergen, Kenneth J. 1995. Relational theory and the discourses of power. In *Management and organization: Relational alternatives to individualism,* edited by Dian Marie Hosking, H. Peter Dachler, and Kenneth J. Gergen. Aldershot, UK: Avebury.

Gergen, Kenneth J. 2009a. *An invitation to social construction.* London: Sage Publications.

Gergen, Kenneth J. 2009b. *Relational being.* Oxford: Oxford University Press.

Gergen, Kenneth J., and Mary Gergen. 2003. *Social construction: A reader.* London: Sage Publications.

Gergen, Kenneth J., A. Gulerce, Andy Lock, and G. Misra. 1996. Psychological science in cultural context. *American Psychologist* 51 (5):496–503.

Gergen, Kenneth J., and Sheila McNamee. 2000. From disordered to generative dialogues. In *The construction of disorder,* edited by R. Neimeyer and J. D. Raskin. Washington, DC: American Psychological Association.

Gergen, Kenneth J., Sheila McNamee, and Frank J. Barrett. 2001. Toward transformative dialogue. *International Journal of Public Administration* 24 (7/8):679–707.

Gergen, Kenneth J., and Tojo Thatchenkery. 1996. Organizational science in a postmodern context. *Journal of Applied Behavioral Science* 32:356–378.

Gergen, M. M., and K. J. Gergen. 1995. What is this thing called love? Emotional scenarios in historical perspective. *Journal of Narrative and Life History* 5 (3):221–237.

Gill, P. 2001. Narrative inquiry: Designing the processes, pathways and patterns of change. *Systems Research and Behavioural Science* 18:335–344.

Graves, Robert. 1986. *Selected poems, The Penguin poets.* (Paul O'Prey, Ed.) New York: Penguin Books.

Greenwood, R., W. Whyte, and I. Harkavy. 1993. Participatory action research as process and as goal. *Human Relations* 46 (2):175–192.

Guba, E. G., and Y. S. Lincoln. 1989. *Fourth generation evaluation.* Newbury Park, CA: Sage Publications.

Guba, E.G. and Y.S. Lincoln. 1994. Competing paradigms in qualitative research. In *Handbook of qualitative research*, edited by N. Denzin and Y. Lincoln. London: Sage Publications.

Haar, Dorieke van der, and Dian Marie Hosking. 2004. Evaluating appreciative inquiry: A relational constructionist approach. *Human Relations* 57 (8):1017–1036.

Harding, Sandra. 1986. *The science question in feminism.* Milton Keyes: Open University Press.

Harding, Sandra. 1998. *Is science multicultural?* Bloomington, IN: Indiana University Press.

Hardy, C., N. Phillips, and S. Clegg. 2001. Reflexivity in organization and management theory: A study of the production of the research 'subject.' *Human Relations* 54 (5):531–560.

Hassard, John. 1991. Multiple paradigms and organizational analysis: A case study. *Organization Studies* 12 (2):275–299.

Hermans, H. J. M., H. J. G. Kempen, and R. J. P. Van Loon. 1992. The dialogical self: Beyond individualism and rationalism. *American Psychologist* 47 (1):23–33.

Heron, John. 1996. *Cooperative inquiry.* London: Sage.

Hicks, Jeff. 2010. *Co-constructive consulting: A pragmatic, relational constructionist approach.* Twente, The Netherlands: University of Twente Press.

Hoeg, Peter. 1994. *Borderliners.* London: The Harvill Press.

Hollis, Martin. 1994. *The philosophy of social science: An introduction.* Cambridge, UK: Cambridge University Press.

Holstein, J. A., and J. F. Gubrium. 2008. *Handbook of constructionist research.* New York: Guilford.

Holzman, Lois. 1999. *Performing psychology: A postmodern culture of the mind.* New York: Routledge.

Hosking, Dian Marie. 1995. Constructing power: Entitative and relational approaches. In *Management and organization: Relational alternatives to individualism*, edited by D. M. Hosking, H. P. Dachler, and K. J. Gergen. Aldershot, UK: Avebury.

Hosking, Dian Marie. 2000. Ecology in mind, mindful practices. *European Journal of Work and Organizational Psychology* 9 (2):147–158.

Hosking, Dian Marie. 2004. Changeworks: A critical construction. In *Dynamics of organisational change and learning*, edited by J. Boonstra. Chichester: Wiley.

Hosking, Dian Marie. 2006. Not leaders, not followers: A postmodern discourse of leadership processes. In *Follower-centered perspectives on leadership: A tribute to the memory of James R. Meindl*, edited by R. P. Boas Shamir, M. Bligh, and Mary Uhl-Bien. Greenwich, CT: Information Age Publishing.

Hosking, Dian Marie. 2007a. Can constructionism be critical? In *Handbook of constructionist research*, edited by James Holstein and Jaber Gubrium. New York: Guilford Publications.

Hosking, Dian Marie. 2007b. Sound constructs: A constructionist discourse of sound processes and listening. *Revue Sciences de Gestion* 55:55–75.

Hosking, Dian Marie. 2008. Can constructionism be critical? In *Handbook of constructionist research*, edited by J. A. Holstein and J. F. Gubrium. New York: Guilford.

Hosking, Dian Marie. 2010. Moving relationality: Meditations on a relational approach to leadership. In *Sage handbook of leadership*, edited by D. C. Allan Bryman, Keith Grint, Brad Jackson, and Mary Uhl-Bien. London: Sage Publications.

Hosking, Dian Marie. 2011. Telling tales of relations: Appreciating relational constructionism. *Organization Studies* 32 (1):47–65.

Hosking, Dian Marie, and Sheila McNamee, eds. 2006. *The social construction of organization*. Herndon, VA: Copenhagen Business School Press.

Hosking, Dian Marie, and Sheila McNamee. 2007, November. Back to basics: Appreciating appreciative inquiry as not 'normal' science. *AIPractitioner*, pp. 12–16.

Hosking, Dian Marie, and Ian E. Morley. 1991. *A social psychology of organising*. Chichester: Harvester Wheatsheaf.

Hosking, Dian Marie, and Ian E. Morley. 2004. Social constructionism in community and applied social psychology. *Journal of Community & Applied Social Psychology* 14 (5):318–331.

Hosking, Dian Marie and Bettina Pluut. 2010. (Re)constructing reflexivity: A relational constructionist approach. *The Qualitative Report* 15 (1).

Howard, G. S. 1991. A narrative approach to thinking, cross-cultural psychology, and psychotherapy. *American Psychologist* 46 (3):187–197.

Howeling, Loes. 2011. *Let's dance: Narratives about boundaries in teacher-student relations: A self-other ethnography on learning and teaching*. Unpublished doctoral dissertation, Utrecht: University for Humanistics.

Isaacs, William. 1993. Taking flight: Dialogue, collective thinking and organizational learning. *Organizational Dynamics* 22 (2):24–39.

Isaacs, William. 2001. Toward an action theory of dialogue. *International Journal of Public Administration* 24 (7/8):709–748.

Jaworski, Joseph, and Betty Flowers. 1998. *Synchronicity: The inner path of leadership*. San Francisco: Berrett-Koehler.

Kerlinger, Fred N. 1964. *Foundations of behavioral research: Educational and psychological inquiry*. New York: Holt.

Kleisterlee, Ernst, and Dian Marie Hosking. 2009. Centering the path. *CMS Conference*. Warwick University, available at: /www.relational-constructionism.org/pages/publications/articles.php

Korzybski, A. 1933. *Science and sanity: An introduction to non-Aristotelian systems and general semantics*. Englewood, NJ: Institute of General Semantics.

Kuhn, Thomas S. 1970. *The structure of scientific revolutions*. Chicago: University of Chicago Press.

Kutchins, Herb, and Stuart A. Kirk. 1997. *Making us crazy: DSM: The psychiatric bible and the creation of mental disorders*. New York: Free Press.

Kvale, Steiner. 2008. *InterViews: An introduction to qualitative research interviewing*. London: Sage Publications.

Lakoff, G. and M. Johnson. 1980. *Metaphors we live by*. Chicago: University of Chicago Press.

Lakoff, G., and M. Johnson. 1999. *Philosophy in the flesh: The embodied mind and its challenge to western thought*. New York: Basic Books.

Lannamann, John W. 1998a. The place of the constructed in a materially responsive world. *Family Process* 37 (4):421–423.

Lannamann, John W. 1998b. Social construction and materiality: The limits of indeterminacy in therapeutic settings. *Family Process* 37 (4):393–413.

Latour, Bruno. 1986. People, science and technology. *Technology and Culture* 27 (4):910–911.

Latour, Bruno. 1987. *Science in action: How to follow scientists and engineers through society.* Cambridge, MA: Harvard University Press.

Latour, Bruno, and Stephen Woolgar. 1979. *Laboratory life: The social construction of scientific facts.* London: Sage Publications.

Levinas, Emmanual. 1985. *Ethics and infinity.* Translated by R. A. Cohen. Pittsburgh: Duquesne University Press.

Lewis, M., and Keleman, M. 2002. Mutiparadigm inquiry: Exploring organizational pluralism and paradox. *Human Relations* 55 (2):251–275.

Madison, D. Soyini. 2005. *Critical ethnography: Methods, ethics and performance.* London: Sage Publications.

McNamee, Sheila. 1988. Accepting research as social intervention: Implications of a systemic epistemology. *Communication Quarterly* 36 (1):50–68.

McNamee, Sheila. 1994. Research as relationally situated activity: Ethical implications. *Journal of Feminist Family Therapy* 6 (3):69–83.

McNamee, Sheila. 1998. Reinscribing organizational wisdom and courage: The relationally engaged organization. In *Organizational wisdom and executive courage,* edited by S. Srivastva and D. Cooperrider. San Francisco: The New Lexington Press.

McNamee, Sheila. 2004a. Appreciative evaluation within a conflicted educational context. *New Directions in Evaluation* 100:23–40.

McNamee, Sheila. 2004b. Critical moments as "transformations." *Negotiation Journal* 20 (2):269–274.

McNamee, Sheila. 2004c. Imagine Chicago: A methodology for cultivating community social construction in practice. *Journal of Community & Applied Social Psychology* 14 (5):406–409.

McNamee, Sheila. 2004d. Promiscuity in the practice of family therapy. *Journal of Family Therapy* 26 (3):224–244.

McNamee, Sheila, and Kenneth J. Gergen. 1992. *Therapy as social construction.* London: Sage Publications.

McNamee, Sheila, and Kenneth J. Gergen. 1999. *Relational responsibility: Resources for sustainable dialogue.* Thousand Oaks, CA: Sage.

Mir, R., and A. Mir. 2002. The organizational imagination: From paradigm wars to praxis. *Organizational Research Methods* 5:105–125.

Morgan, Gareth. 1986. *Images of organisation.* London: Sage.

Morgan, Gareth. 1997. *Imaginization.* London: Sage.

New Economics Foundation. 1998. *Participation works* [cited March 5, 2010]. Available at http://www.neweconimcs.org/publications/participation-works.

Newman, Fred, and Lois Holzman. 1997. *The end of knowing: A new developmental way of learning.* New York: Routledge.

Nichol, Lee. 2004. Forward. In *On dialogue,* edited by D. Bohm. London: Routledge.

Oxford English Dictionary. 2010. Oxford: Oxford University Press.

Palmer, Ian, and Ricky Dunford. 1996. Conflicting uses of metaphors: Reconceptualizing their use in the field of organisational change. *Academy of Management Review* 21 (3):691–717.

Parker, Ian. 2005. *Qualitative psychology: Introducing radical research.* Buckingham: Open University Press.

Pearce, W. Barnett. 1992. A 'camper's guide' to constructionisms. *Human Systems: The Journal of Systemic Consultation and Management* 3:139–161.

Potter, Jonathan, and A. Hepburn. 2008. Discursive constructionism. In *Handbook of constructionist research*, edited by J. A. Holstein and J. F. Gubrium. New York: Guilford.

Potter, Jonathan, and Margaret Wetherell. 1987. *Discourse and social psychology: Beyond attitudes and behaviour.* London: Sage Publications.

Putnam, Hilary. 1990. *Realism with a human face.* Cambridge, MA: Harvard University Press.

Reason, Peter. 1994. *Participation in human inquiry.* London: Sage Publications.

Reason, Peter, and Hilary Bradbury, eds. 2001. *Handbook of action research: Participative inquiry and practice.* London: Sage Publications.

Reason, Peter, and William Torbert. 2001. The action turn: Towards a transformational social science. *Concepts and Transformation* 6 (1):1–37.

Reed, Jan. 2007. *Appreciative inquiry: Research for change.* London: Sage Publications.

Rhodes, Carl, and Andrew D. Brown. 2005. Writing responsibly: Narrative fiction and organization. *Organization* 12 (4):467–491.

Riessman, Catherine K. 1993. *Narrative analysis.* Newbury Park, CA: Sage Publications.

Rogoff, Barbara, Carolyn Goodman Turkanis, and Leslee Bartlett, eds. 2001. *Learning together: Children and adults in a school community.* Oxford: Oxford University Press.

Roth, Sallyann, Laura Chasin, Richard Chasin, Carol Becker, and Margaret Herzig. 1992. From debate to dialogue: A facilitating role for family therapists in the public forum. *Dulwich Centre Newsletter* 2:41–48.

Saha, Shayamal Kumar. 2009. *Promotion of self-help in development & social change.* Unpublished doctoral dissertation, University of Tilburg.

Sampson, Edward E. 1993. *Celebrating the other: A dialogic account of human nature.* Boulder, CO: Westview Press.

Sarbin, T. 1986. *Narrative psychology: The storied nature of human conduct.* New York: Praeger.

Schön, Donald A. 1983. *The reflective practitioner: How professionals think in action.* New York: Basic Books.

Schultz, Majken, and Mary Jo Hatch. 1996. Living with multiple paradigms: The case of paradigm interplay in organizational culture studies. *Academy of Management Review* 21 (2):529–557.

Selvini, Mara, Luigi Boscolo, Gianfranco Cecchin, and Guiliana Prata. 1980. Hypothesizing—circularity—neutrality. *Family Process* 19:73–85.

Senge, Peter. 1990. *The fifth discipline: The art and practice of the learning organization.* New York: Doubleday.

Senge, Peter. 2004. Preface. In *On dialogue*, edited by D. Bohm. London: Routledge.

Senge, Peter, Claus Otto Scharmer, Joseph Jaworski, and Betty Flowers. 2005. *Presence: Exploring profound change in people, organizations, and society.* New York: Doubleday.

Shotter, John D. 2001. Participative thinking: "Seeing the face" and "hearing the voice" of social situations. *Career Development International* 6 (7):343–347.

Shotter, John D. 2010. *Social construction on the edge: 'Withness' thinking and embodiment.* Chagrin Falls, OH: Taos Institute Publications.

Shotter, John D., and Arlene M. Katz. 1999. 'Living moments' in dialogical exchanges. *Human Systems: The Journal of Systemic Consultation and Management* 9:81–93.

Silverman, David. 2010. *Doing qualitative research: A practical handbook*, 3rd ed. London: Sage.

Stake, Robert E. 1975. *Evaluating the arts in education: A responsive approach.* Columbus, OH: Merrill.

Stenner, P., and C. Eccleston. 1994. On the textuality of being. *Theory and Psychology* 4 (1):85–103.

Swanborn, P. G. 1999. *Evalueren: Het ontwerpen, begeleiden en evalueren van interventies.* Amsterdam: Boom.

Thomas, Jim. 1993. *Doing critical ethnography.* London: Sage Publications.

Tillmann-Healy, Lisa M. 1996. A secret life in a culture of thinness. In *Composing ethnography*, edited by C. Ellis and A. P. Bochner. Walnut Creek, CA: AltaMira.

Tomm, Karl. 1985. Circular interviewing: A multifaceted clinical tool. In *Applications of system family therapy: The Milan method*, edited by D. Campbell and R. Draper. New York: Grune and Stratton.

Torbert, William. 2000. The practice of action inquiry. In *Handbook of action research: Participative inquiry and practice*, edited by P. Reason and H. Bradbury. London: Sage.

Toulmin, Stephen, and Bjorn Gustavsen. 1996. *Beyond theory: Changing organizations through participation.* Amsterdam: Benjamins.

Uhl-Bien, Mary. 2004. Relational leadership approaches. In *Encyclopedia of leadership*, edited by G.R. Goethals, G.J. Sorenson, and J. M. Burns. Los Angeles: Sage.

Uhl-Bien, Mary. 2006. Relational leadership theory: Exploring the social processes of leadership and organizing. *The Leadership Quarterly* 17:654–676.

van Dijk, Teun. 2008. *Discourse and context: A sociocognitive approach.* Cambridge, UK: Cambridge University Press.

Vygotsky, L.S. 1978. *Mind in society.* Cambridge, MA: Harvard University Press.

Watzlawick, Paul, Janet Beavin Bavelas, and Don D. Jackson. 1967. *Pragmatics of human communication: A study of interactional patterns, pathologies, and paradoxes.* New York: Norton.

Watzlawick, Paul, John H. Weakland, and Richard Fisch. 1974. *Change: Principles of problem formation and problem resolution.* New York: Norton.

Weinberg, Darin. 2008. The philosophical foundations of constructionist research. In *Handbook of constructionist research*, edited by James A. Holstein and Jaber F. Gubrium. New York: Guilford Press.

Weisbord, Marvin R., and Sandra Janoff. 1995. *Future search: An action guide to finding common ground in organizations and communities.* San Francisco: Berrett-Koehler.

Weisbord, Marvin R., and Sandra Janov. 2000. *Collaborating for change: Future search.* San Francisco: Berrett-Kohler.

White, Michael, and David Epston. 1990. *Narrative means to therapeutic ends.* New York: Norton.

Wittgenstein, Ludwig. 1953. *Philosophical investigations.* Oxford: B. Blackwell.

Wood, Julia T. 2004. Forward: Entering into dialogue. In *Dialogue: Theorizing difference in communication studies*, edited by R. Anderson, L. A. Baxter, and K. N. Cissna. Thousand Oaks, CA: Sage Publications.

Woolgar, Steve, ed. 1996. *Psychology, qualitative methods and the ideas of science.* Leicester: BPS Publications.

Index

Senge, Peter, 68, 130
Shotter, John, 47, 77, 104, 116, 119, 130
social science perspectives. *See* meta-theories

T

theory: role of, 42–43
transformative, 1; inquiry as, 10–11, 61; orienting themes, 73–77. *See* dialogue; participation

V

valuing: fact and value, 14,79,97–100; always ongoing, 79–83; intervention and, 82; ethics and, 105. *See also* evaluation as method

W

Wittgenstein, Ludwig, xiii, xv, 6, 31, 34, 37, 43, 57, 101, 110, 131
Woolgar, Steve, 19–24, 34, 38, 117, 129, 131

Made in the USA
Lexington, KY
05 May 2018